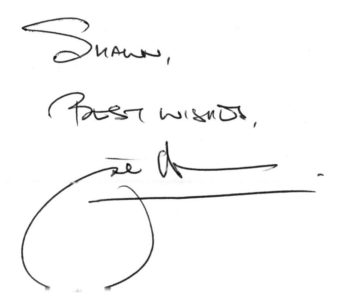

Shawn,

Best wishes,

Also by Dr. Joe MacInnis

DEEP
LEADERSHIP

ESSENTIAL INSIGHTS FROM HIGH-RISK ENVIRONMENTS

DR. JOE MacINNIS

Alfred A. Knopf Canada

LIBRARY AND ARCHIVES CANADA CATALOGUING IN PUBLICATION

MacInnis, Joe, 1937–
Deep leadership: Essential Insights from High-Risk Environments / Joe MacInnis.

Issued also in electronic format.

ISBN 978-0-307-36110-3

1. Leadership. 2. MacInnis, Joe, 1937– —Anecdotes. I. Title.

HM1261.M33 2012   303.3'4   C2011-904640-7

Cover and text design by Andrew Roberts
Cover image: Jeff Rotman/Digital Vision/Getty Images

Printed and bound in the United States of America

10 9 8 7 6 5 4 3 2 1

CONTENTS

Jim Cameron on the deck of the ship EDT *Ares*.

SEARCHING FOR THE ESSENCE OF LEADERSHIP

JAMES CAMERON, the acclaimed Hollywood director, applies his leadership skills in the most intriguing places. I've seen him choreographing actors, lighting experts, and computer operators on the set of *Avatar* in Los Angeles. I've watched him coordinate scientists, cameramen, and sub-pilots on research ships in the North Atlantic. But in 2010, in a third floor conference room in the EPA building in Washington, I saw him confront a different kind of challenge.

The rectangular room had cherrywood walls, big-frame video screens, and sunlight streaming through a south-facing window. There were twenty-two men and women, sitting around a long table with laptop computers open in front of us. Dressed in a blue open-collar shirt, Cameron welcomed us to the meeting.

"Thanks for coming and spending the day with us. Thanks for taking the time to brainstorm a really tough problem."

The problem was Deepwater Horizon, a runaway oil well five thousand feet under the ocean. After repeated attempts, the four companies responsible for the blowout had failed to cap the well. Millions of barrels of oil had escaped and the northeast section of the Gulf of Mexico was turning into a biological black hole.

Around the table were deep-sea experts from Woods Hole Oceanographic, Harbor Branch Oceanographic, NOAA, the University of California, and the Russian Academy of Sciences. They were men and women who had logged hundreds of hours beneath the sea at depths greater than five thousand feet and could easily imagine what was taking place beneath the surface of the Gulf.

It was a great dying that no one could see. Hundreds of cubic miles of seawater were filling with ragged black columns, thick streams, and small droplets of oil. For weeks, an enormous, expanding fog of oil had been enveloping the larvae and newborn of snapper, dolphin, lobster, billfish, and bluefin tuna.

The prodigy of death and mutilations in young and mature animals included eye wounds, gill wounds, stomach wounds, gelatinous tissue wounds, and oxygen-deprived metabolisms.

The killing continued right up to the surface where phytoplankton—the lungs of the planet—were savaged by the violence of the oil and the chemicals used to disperse it. Trillions and trillions of dead microorganisms rained down through the filthy procession of upward-moving oil. In deep water they merged with the uncounted corpses of crustaceans and in deeper water still, the remnants of big fish, small fish, turtles and invertebrates. The deluge of megadeath continued until the lifeless remains came to rest on the brown floor of the Gulf.

Unprepared for what was happening beneath their ships, senior managers were slow to respond. Their hapless attempts to contain the well included the deployment of a useless four-storey containment vessel and a bizarre "top-kill" operation using golf balls and mud. Tony Hayward, BP's CEO, was saying all the wrong things: "The environmental impact is likely to be very, very modest," he whispered hoarsely at an early news conference. A few weeks later he remarked, "Nobody wants this over more than I do. I want my life back."

The stark truth was that BP had no emergency plan for the worst environmental disaster in American history. There were no containment systems and no rapid response teams ready to deal with such an unprecedented event. There was a severe lack of strategic leadership.

"BP has a hundred engineers working on this," continued Cameron, "so it's unlikely we'll come up with technical options they haven't thought of. But we owe it to ourselves, and the ocean, to do some hard thinking about future responses of the scientific community."

No one in the room had more time inside the confines of a research sub than Cameron. He'd made seventy-two dives to hydrothermal vent systems, the *Titanic*, and the *Bismarck*, a shipwreck three times as deep as the runaway well. He was on intimate terms with the lethal forces of the deep sea including unpredictable currents, near-freezing temperatures, everlasting darkness, and pressures that bend steel.

Cameron had selected us with the same kind of care that went into his six major deep-sea expeditions to the Atlantic and Pacific Oceans. We represented a wide range of disciplines—marine engineering, marine biology, diving medicine, deep-sea imaging—and we knew more about our subjects than he did. We were comfortable with lateral thinking and wouldn't hesitate to tell him if he was wrong.

Cameron selected us because we'd spent years thinking "inside" the ocean. Men from BP, Transocean, and Halliburton—oilmen operating in air-conditioned workrooms on surface vessels—thought exclusively in oil terms, but we worked with research subs and remotely piloted vehicles miles beneath the surface. We were scientists who thought in scientific terms.

I WAS in Washington with two objectives: the first was to contribute to the discussion and help write the report for senior government officials at EPA, the Department of Energy, NOAA, and the US Coast Guard. Before the day was over I would write the opening words of *Considering Technical Options for Controlling the BP Blowout in the Gulf of Mexico*.

But I had another objective: the workshop was an open window on the subject of leadership. When you spend a lifetime studying people who influence other people, Cameron was the kind of man who held your attention. His Hollywood films had won twenty-one Academy Awards. He was an acclaimed deep-sea explorer, inventor, and businessman. Well before the release of *Avatar*, he was an ardent earth activist.

My first contact with Cameron was a few weeks before Buzz Aldrin and Neil Armstrong put their historic bootprints on the moon. Using a research grant from *National Geographic*, I had just built a sixteen-foot-high underwater station to study the interior of Lake Huron. Before we placed it on the lakebed, it was displayed outside Toronto's Royal Ontario Museum. One morning a fifteen-year-old Jim Cameron stepped out of a school bus, saw its living chamber and four view ports and wrote me a letter asking for details about its construction. He and his brother Mike built a small model of their own, put a mouse inside, and successfully tested it in a river near their home.

I've followed the astonishing arc of his professional life ever since: the long road from Niagara Falls, Ontario, to Hollywood, California, and the breakthrough films including *The Terminator* and *Titanic*; the financial success and Academy Awards; and, since 1995, a second career exploring the deep ocean. As a participant in his last two expeditions for *Disney* and the *Discovery Channel*, I had seen him direct ships, research subs, remotely operated vehicles and hundreds of men and women from ten universities, the Russian Academy of Sciences, and NASA.

But when he called us together for the meeting in Washington he was demonstrating yet another dimension of leadership: the ability to take charge when unexpected circumstances demand it. Angered by a runaway oil well on an already overstressed ocean, he was using his financial and intellectual resources to try to protect a planet in peril.

THIS BOOK is for people who find themselves in a position of leadership and want to know more about the structure and dynamics of their new role. *Deep Leadership* draws on years of field work and more than five thousand hours under the Atlantic, Pacific, and Arctic Oceans. It's rooted in the time I've spent with men and women who lead teams using complex equipment in life-threatening environments: marine scientists who use twenty-million-dollar research subs to study the ocean's greatest depths, shuttle astronauts who orbited the earth at 28,000 kilometres per hour while constructing the International Space Station, soldiers and pilots fighting the Taliban in Afghanistan, and women who serve on combat warships.

My trip to Afghanistan was a critical step in the making of this book. As I was writing it I realized I needed to know more about warrior leadership, especially as it was being used in asymmetrical warfare. With the support of Colonel Bill Bentley, director of the Canadian Forces Leadership Institute, I spent time on a combat warship in the Caribbean Sea and flew to the Canadian Forces military base in Kandahar, Afghanistan. Along the way, I interviewed forty-two men and women, of all ranks, in the army, navy, air force and special forces. In the cockpits of their aircraft, the front seats of their armoured vehicles and on the bridge of HMCS *Toronto*, they talked about leadership critical moments. They described the skills and qualities needed for twenty-first-century military leadership and how these attributes are acquired. They talked about courage, compassion, and the critical importance of mentoring young leaders.

Leadership is a subject I've been trying to understand since I was a medical student at the University of Toronto. I study it because it's how we solve our professional and political problems. It defines how we work together and how we're going to deal with global challenges like the climate crisis, cyberwarfare, food shortages, and failed states.

To better understand the significance of these social and planetary issues, I sought out activists like Thomas Homer-Dixon, Margaret Atwood, Pete Seeger, and Jane Goodall. Listening to their words and reading their books helped enlarge my concept of "deep leadership."

DURING MY long career I've had more than my share of leadership luck. Edwin Link, the man who gave me my first job, was an alpha influencer. Pierre Trudeau, Walter Cronkite, Jacques Cousteau, and Scott Carpenter were among my early leadership mentors. Quite by chance, my ambition to lead undersea expeditions to the Arctic was enhanced by Canada's first national ocean policy. Whenever I probe my own biography it's clear that I'm an accidental leader.

This book relies on the efforts of many others. I've been informed by a wide variety of sources including literary fiction, non-fiction, scientific journals, and the *New York Times*. The core contributions come from courageous, multidisciplined people who shared their ideas during hard projects and challenging conversations.

Readers of my previous books will find that I've borrowed heavily from my early work. Sometimes it takes years to understand what you learned from an event or a mentor.

Leadership is complex and multilayered, and covers a wide spectrum from personal to professional and political. It has a long shadow; nothing succeeds without it. Our struggle to find new leaders defines some of history's most dramatic moments. Think of the election of Barack Obama or the recent struggles in countries like Egypt, Libya, and Syria.

Some leadership traits are easy to see; others lie beneath the surface. How they're applied—alone or synchronized—over a period of time determines the success of the leader. With time, talent, and tenacity, leadership can be learned. That's the project of this book: one that I will relate in three sections. First I'll describe my lifelong and still emerging relationship with leadership. In the second, I'll highlight what I consider to be the twelve essential traits of leadership, and show you how to identify them, appreciate them, and emulate them. Finally, in the third section, I'll show you how your own leadership journey can begin (or begin again) by making the commitment, commanding the language, building a library, finding mentors, and actively seeking leadership opportunities.

My leadership search has taken me from Washington to Moscow and from the North Pole to Antarctica. Along the way I've shared insights with some extraordinary people. The clarity of their ideas and the grace of their actions can help you make one of the most fascinating human journeys—becoming a strategic thinker who looks into the future, makes the right choices, and inspires others to follow.

PART ONE: A PERSONAL JOURNEY

The author and Corporal Amy Roddy in Kandahar, Afghanistan.

IN APRIL 1963 I was a junior intern at Toronto's Sick Children Hospital coming off an all-night shift in the emergency department. As I stepped inside the cafeteria wondering if I had enough energy to eat breakfast, I glanced at the front page of the morning newspaper and felt a measure of dread. One of the headlines said that an American nuclear submarine making a test dive had been lost with all hands in the North Atlantic. The story reported that the US Department of the Navy would gather a panel of experts to review the cause of the accident and the operational readiness of its undersea fleet. I wasn't aware of it at the time, but the tragic loss of the USS *Thresher* would initiate my career in undersea medical research and make me an accidental apprentice on the road to leadership.

Six years later, the USS *Manhattan*, an American oil tanker, steamed through the Northwest Passage with the assistance of an icebreaker, to confirm that this remote, ice-covered route could be used to transport oil from Alaska. Government officials in Ottawa wrote urgent reports about the impact of an oil spill on the nation's northern coastline and Canadian sovereignty. Once again, an event thousands of miles away changed my life. The same officials encouraged me to lead a series of research expeditions under the ice of the Northwest Passage, and suddenly, I found myself an accidental leader.

In 1989, a top-secret Russian nuclear attack submarine caught fire crossing the Norwegian Sea and sank with the loss of forty-two men. Marine scientists were alarmed about the possible environmental impact of the sub's reactor and nuclear torpedoes. At the time, I was working with the Russian scientists who used their research subs to survey the wreck. Their stories and video images opened my eyes to the dangers of runaway radioactivity and started me thinking about the increasing stresses on our planetary and social systems. Wondering if what

I was learning about leadership in lethal environments might help diminish some of these stresses, I became a serious student of leadership.

Three ships in three oceans, and the events that followed, form the headwaters of this book. Here's how it all happened.

The author and his team partners on *Deep Diver*.

ACCIDENTAL APPRENTICE

IN APRIL 1963 the USS *Thresher*, a three-hundred-foot, nuclear-powered, fast-attack submarine, sailed out of New Hampshire's Portsmouth Naval Shipyard. Inside her huge pressure hull were 16 officers, 96 sailors, and 17 men from the shipyard. *Thresher* was a lethal machine of the Cold War, one of thousands that included strategic bombers and land-based missiles built by the United States and the Soviet Union.

Until nuclear power came along, military submarines were limited to the upper few hundred feet of the ocean. Now they could range to depths five times as deep, pushing their long, black hulls into an unknown universe.

Thresher's massive hull was a series of steel rings and two end domes welded together into a single unit. It was designed to operate safely only to a depth of a thousand feet. At 1,500 feet—called the "crush depth"—it would rupture.

One hundred and ninety nautical miles east of Cape Cod, *Thresher* began a test dive that would take her to her maximum operating depth. Throughout the length of the submarine from the torpedo room to the wardroom, and from the reactor compartment to the main engine room, groups of men studied instruments and dials. The officers were experts in physics, electrical engineering, heat transfer, reactor theory, and radiological control. The members of the crew were among the most carefully selected and best trained in the United States Navy.

WITHOUT WARNING there was a hard, sharp sound in a machinery space near the reactor. A narrow pipe filled with seawater burst open. As word of the emergency spread through the three-storey vessel, men rushed to repair the damage, but the cold water pouring out of the pipe filled the room with a freezing fog, tearing out wires, flooding control panels, and short-circuiting electrical switches. Circuit breakers tripped. Panels went dead. Officers called out hoarse commands. Sailors acknowledged the commands and responded with rapid movements.

Minutes later, *Thresher*'s nuclear reactor shut down, her turbines lost steam and the four-thousand-ton sub slowed to a stop, stalled, and then began to slide backwards toward the centre of the earth.

Inside the blackness, *Thresher* descended through gathering pressures. Somewhere below her crush depth, driven by the weight of half a mile of water, the ocean slammed through a section of her hull. The thunderous explosion broke *Thresher* into three large pieces and hundreds of smaller ones. The pieces fell until they came to rest on a seafloor more than eight thousand feet deep.

In low-ceilinged, fluorescent-lit rooms within the Pentagon and Kremlin, naval scientists bent over notepads and wrote memoranda to senior officers. They described the size and shape of *Thresher*'s nuclear reactor and speculated about its final position on the seafloor. Men who'd written orders for the dumping of thousands of drums of low-level radioactive waste in submerged canyons off Kamchatka and the Farallon Islands wondered what a highly radioactive fire burning for twenty thousand years might do to the integrity of the ocean.

Two weeks after the disaster, the Secretary of the Navy brought together a panel of experts in underwater engineering and submarine operations to study the accident, assess the navy's deep-sea capabilities and make recommendations. Heading the panel's civilian sector was the wealthy businessman, philanthropist, and undersea pioneer Edwin A. Link—the first of my many leadership mentors.

"**WHEN DID** you make your first dive under the ocean?" Link asked me.

I squirmed in the hard wooden chair. Five months after the disaster, I was sitting in a small, book-filled office at the Washington Navy Yard answering questions from this straight-shouldered man in his late fifties. Ed Link was of medium height with thick-rimmed glasses. The buckshot gleam in his eyes said he didn't suffer fools. I was twenty-six years old and after four years of medical school and a year of internship, desperately looking for work. My only assets were a burning enthusiasm for undersea exploration and a willingness to learn.

"I was eighteen, sir," I said. "At a competitive swimming meet in Fort Lauderdale when someone suggested we explore the near shore reef. I got checked out in the pool in the morning and made a sixty-foot scuba dive in the afternoon." Link stared at me without blinking; I flushed with sweat.

As the "father" of the simulation industry, Link had a dense web of interconnected skills and a learn-by-doing approach to life. Born in Binghamton, New York, he had begun his career when aviation was changing from conquest of the air to an essential, high-risk mail service. He became a pilot at a time when the rules of flying were made up in the cockpit and dozens of young men were slamming into the earth. Concerned about the mounting fatalities, Link set about inventing a device to teach pilots how to fly while still safely on the ground. It took him three years of trial and error, many sleepless nights, and significant financial brinkmanship before he came up with a prototype flight simulator. During the Second World War, the "Link trainer" became a rapidly expanding commercial enterprise; advanced versions saved thousands of lives and led to dramatic improvements in instrument flying and navigation techniques. Now, in 1963, the companies he had founded were building complex, two-storey simulators for commercial airline pilots and Mercury and Gemini astronauts.

Link leveraged his business acumen into strategic philanthropy. He established the Link Foundation to provide financial assistance for young men and women seeking careers in science and engineering. Unsatisfied with the diminishing returns of corporate life, he began to invent machines to explore the oceans. He created partnerships with the Smithsonian Institution and the National Geographic Society and built a state-of-the-art research ship called *Sea Diver*.

A year earlier, supported by the US Navy's Sixth Fleet, he had tested his new diving chamber by lowering it into the sea and suspending it sixty feet beneath his ship. He dived down to it, swam up through a bottom hatch, and remained inside for a full six hours, all the while breathing a synthetic mixture of oxygen and helium. The helium changed the sound of his voice and made him shiver with cold, but he now had the confidence to go much deeper.

"You invested four years in medical school," Link continued. "Were you a good student?"

I hesitated. "To be honest sir, I was interested in other things."

Link pondered this, closed his eyes and clasped his hands an inch in front of his nose. I was convinced he was deciding how to let me down gracefully.

"Would you like to see our ship?" he asked instead.

We left the office and walked past a row of navy vessels moored against the bright sheen of the Anacostia River. Link stopped in front of a 110-foot research ship with a white hull and *Sea Diver* painted on her stern. Halfway up her gangway he paused. "I was bored so I left high school after my junior year," he said. "It was a good move. By not going to university, I failed to learn my limitations."

A month later, I received a Link Foundation Fellowship to study diving medicine at the University of Pennsylvania. In Philadelphia, Washington, and Key West, I would work with US Navy divers and test the oxygen and carbon dioxide monitors we would use in Link's next deep dive.

THE FOLLOWING July I joined Ed Link and his team on *Sea Diver* in Miami. We powered across the Gulf Stream and dropped anchor just north of Great Stirrup Cay in the Bahamas. Assisted by the US Navy support vessel *Nahant* we lowered a small station to a depth of 432 feet.

For six months we had been preparing Robert Stenuit and his co-diver Jon Lindberg for the "longest-deepest dive" in human history. Far from the reach of surface divers, they would face a lethal constellation of hazards including hypothermia, gas embolism, decompression sickness, and oxygen poisoning. New breathing devices, thermal suits, and a decompression chamber were built and tested. We made sure both men were physically and medically fit and ran them through two simulated "dry" dives.

Even before Stenuit and Lindbergh took up residence in their small "house" at 432 feet they were breathing an exotic mixture of oxygen and helium. For the next forty-nine hours Dr. Jim Dickson and I used closed-circuit television to monitor every word and gesture. We watched them drop into the exit hatch and swim outside in the near-freezing waters to make observations and take pictures. We saw them sleep fitfully in their bunks. We advised them on the oxygen, helium, and carbon dioxide levels inside the station and saw them struggle (with trembling hands) to fix a failed electrical system and a non-functioning gas filter. Throughout it all, Ed Link stood next to us offering advice and support. He was a tower of strength and tight-lipped optimism. After five days of carefully controlled decompression, we returned both divers safely to the surface.

After the record-breaking dive, Link and his business partners including the Singer Corporation and Union Carbide formed a new undersea engineering company: Ocean Systems Inc. They soon had contracts with the US Navy, the Office of Naval Research, Exxon, and Shell. As the company's medical director, I was responsible for the health and safety of seventy commercial divers working on offshore oil platforms and pipelines in the Gulf of Mexico, the Santa Barbara Channel, and the North Sea. It was a lot of responsibility for an accidental apprentice.

Ed Link and his partners built new diving bells and research subs and gave us the time and financial support to test them to their limits. With his encouragement Ocean Systems participated in challenging deep-sea operations from the recovery of an H-bomb in three thousand feet of water off the coast of Spain to the salvage of a B-52 that crashed into Lake Michigan. Link and the senior managers of Ocean Systems told us what to do and then gave us the room and resources to do it. We were allowed to take chances and make mistakes—as long as they were small mistakes and we didn't repeat them.

Link had a nonacademic, skeptical nature with a deep disdain for the sterile nature of classroom knowledge and how it could get in the way of what was really going on. Intensely curious about the physical forces of the ocean — the wind, waves, currents and pressures — and constantly inventing practical ways of navigating through them, he was the father of his own erudition. In some ways, he was more scientific than many scientists.

Link was also modest about his fame. He was a reluctant writer and uncomfortable speaking to large crowds, but he was physically tough, mentally resilient and blessed with a never-give-up Yankee determination.

Many fascinating people came to his research ship. They included admirals, nuclear submarine officers, and salvage experts. He introduced me to Melville Bell Grosvenor, president of the National Geographic Society, and the German rocket scientist Wernher von Braun. I met the French undersea explorer Jacques Cousteau and US Navy captain George Bond. Cousteau was a master storyteller who used words and images to inspire a love of science and exploration in young people. Bond was a navy research physician who loved literature and the therapy of laughter. Like Link, they were undersea pioneers who lived dangerous, meaningful lives. They had an explorer's mindset and inspired everyone who worked with them and thousands of others who read about their exploits.

But they weren't the only personalities I had the pleasure of meeting. On a hot spring day in Freeport, Grand Bahama, I met an American newscaster who started me thinking about how the media can influence leadership.

"WE'VE GOT a serious problem. My face mask keeps flooding."

I looked at the famous follicles on his upper lip. His moustache was letting water trickle into his mask.

"It's your moustache," I said. "Perhaps we should trim it with a razor."

"That's impossible," he growled. "It's insured for a million dollars."

We were in the Bahamas testing Ed Link's latest invention — a research sub that took four people to the bottom of the ocean and let two of them swim out and work in the depths. A few days before, we'd been told that Walter Cronkite and a CBS News team wanted to film the sub for a series called *The 21st Century*. Link asked me to give Cronkite a medical exam and teach him to dive, so that he could exit the sub at a depth of fifty feet.

"The most trusted man in America" was at the pinnacle of his career, a celebrity anchorman and reporter who'd covered the Normandy invasion, natural disasters, social unrest and the Vietnam War. A nightly presence in twenty-two million American homes, Cronkite spoke in measured sentences calmly describing national and international events from hurricanes to wars to politics. But for all Americans who remember the events of November 21, 1963, he was the consoling voice of a national tragedy.

Late that morning, at the University of Pennsylvania's Medical Sciences building, a colleague stopped me on the stairwell and told me that President Kennedy had been shot. We ran into a nearby room where a dozen people were gathered around a television set. For the next hour we watched CBS News anchorman Walter Cronkite describe the open limousine ride in Dallas, the cheering crowds, the gunfire in front of the book depository and the president slumping forward in his seat. We saw Cronkite slowly take off his black-framed glasses and blink back tears as he said, "President Kennedy died at 1 p.m. Central Standard Time — about one hour ago."

That evening I drove to Washington to pay my respects to a man whose character and leadership were among the reasons I'd come to America. I spent three days on the chilly, shadowed streets near the White House and Lincoln Memorial trying to make sense of what had happened. From a distance, I watched the funeral procession make its way slowly over the bridge to Arlington Cemetery.

To a young Canadian at the beginning of his career (and to thousands of others around the world) President Kennedy was an inspiring figure. He called on young men and women "to bear the burden of a long, twilight struggle . . . against the common enemies . . . of tyranny, poverty, disease and war." One of his first executive orders created the Peace Corps. He took full responsibility for the failure at the Bay of Pigs, stood fast against the Russians in Berlin, and forced the withdrawal of Soviet missiles from Cuba. Determined to see America lead the way in space, he declared, "We choose to go to the moon in this decade and do the other things, not because they are easy, but because they are hard."

I drove back to Philadelphia determined to understand how Kennedy became such a great leader. What qualities made him so inspiring? Was he born with them or did he acquire them? How could I develop similar traits? I was still thinking about such things as I helped Cronkite ready for his dive.

FROM HIS CBS broadcast booth in Florida, describing the pioneering flights of John Glenn and Scott Carpenter, Cronkite had become the resonant voice of the new American space program. As soon as we were introduced, he made it clear he wanted to dive in the sub and would be most displeased if he failed a young doctor's medical exam. "I'm telling a story about America's new frontiers including space and the ocean," he said. "The only way to tell it is from the inside, using the latest technology."

And I had just suggested that he do it without his trademark moustache.

Chuck Peterson, who was taking pictures of Cronkite in the pool, came to my rescue. "Try this, Mr. Cronkite," he said. "It seals the O-rings on my camera and will likely seal your mask." Cronkite spread a thin layer of Vaseline on his moustache, submerged his head, and gave us a thumbs-up.

We spent two hours in the pool going over the equipment he would use and the safety procedures inside the sub. Cronkite was a confident swimmer and looked comfortable in his fins and scuba gear. During the last twenty minutes, he made the pool his own, dropping down to the bottom, inspecting all four corners, pausing at one of its windows to look out at the sunlit lagoon to the west. As we packed up our gear, I asked him what he thought was the most important story of his career. "A century from now," he said, "the story that will be remembered is how humans escaped from their earthly environment and began to live in space and inside the ocean."

The next day Cronkite made his dive out of the sub and reported his story. Like the other programs in the series, it reinforced the core belief that through competence and ingenuity, Americans could master any challenge.

CRONKITE TOLD me it had taken years to develop his competence in front of the camera. As a teenager in Texas he read an article in *Boys' Life* magazine about the adventures of print and radio reporters. It inspired him to work on his high school newspaper and then to study political science and journalism at the University of Texas. After working part time at the *Houston Post*, he left the university to do what he loved best: report on the news. As a reporter for United Press he covered some of the most important events of World War II including the D-Day Invasion, bombing missions over Germany, and the Nuremburg war trials. In the early '50s, as television was beginning to overtake the press and radio as the most important news media, he went to work for CBS.

At first, it was an unlikely fit. "Serious" journalists viewed television with disdain. Radio and print, they contended, were for "real" reporters. In 1961, CBS made Cronkite the anchor of the *CBS Evening News* and two years later, its managing editor. Sixty days after interviewing President Kennedy at the White House, he broke into the program *As The World Turns* to make the fateful announcement that so many of us remember as if it were yesterday. It was a defining moment for Cronkite and the country. Sitting in his shirtsleeves, he captured the struggle for composure that consumed America over the next four days.

Some years later, I picked up a copy of David Halberstam's book *The Powers That Be*. "From his earliest days," Halberstam wrote, "Cronkite was one of the hungriest reporters around, wildly competitive, no one was going to beat him on a story, and as he grew older and more successful, the marvel of it was that he never changed, the wild fires still burned."

Cronkite knew his field, what had been done, what could be done, and the limits. Like any expert, he played the edges. Carefully and courageously he nudged the boundaries to enlarge the role and responsibilities of a news anchor.

A week after the dive, Cronkite sent me a letter of thanks and invited me to visit him at the CBS booth at Cape Canaveral. Just before the launch of Apollo 11 he greeted me inside the glass-walled news van overlooking the launch pad. Talking on his headset, listening to his director, and in front of the cameras, he was a man in his element. Four days later, when Armstrong and Aldrin landed safely on the moon, he made his famous exclamation, "Oh, boy!"

Six months after his dive in the sub, he visited the battlefields in Vietnam and came home to produce a television special. He said the conflict would end as a stalemate and suggested a negotiated peace. In his memoir, A *Reporter's Life*, he quoted Bill Moyers' description of President Johnson's response to the show. "The president flipped off the set and said, 'If I've lost Cronkite, I've lost middle America.'"

As the years passed I kept in touch with him. He wrote the foreword to my book on Arctic undersea research, saying, "There are two great, almost limitless areas where exploration has only begun—the outer space beyond our atmosphere and the inner space below our oceans . . . It is a fascinating, gripping story of man's daring and ingenuity and his heroic willingness to take personal risk to further his knowledge."

Cronkite never stopped being a reporter's reporter. One summer when I was on the North Atlantic on a Russian oceanographic ship, I called him in New York and asked if he'd like to join us for a dive in Bermuda. Two days later, he arrived at the airport. The next morning, he put on a fireproof jumpsuit, climbed into the crew cabin of the research sub, and made the three-thousand-foot descent down the side of the Bermuda seamount. When the hatch opened three hours later, the seventy-three-year-old journalist beamed like a schoolboy. "Spectacular," he said. "I've seen the deep end of a frontier that's fascinated me for decades."

Cronkite had a transformative character. Starting with a limitless sense of wonder about the natural world and the human family, he thought hard about what he was seeing and worked fiercely to compress his thoughts on complex issues into words we could understand. In the process, he transformed himself and all of us who spent time in his company.

Fifteen years later, during a research expedition five hundred miles north of the Arctic Circle, I tried to apply some of things I had learned from him.

The WASP suit inside the dive tent over HMS *Breadalbane*.

ACCIDENTAL LEADER

"IT'S A COMPASS! And right below is the ship's wheel!"

I'd been waiting for years to hear those words. The remotely piloted vehicle panned to the right, shone its lights on the door-frame of the ship's deck house, and returned to the binnacle holding the compass. Slowly it dropped down to reveal the ship's wheel, massive and circular.

Seven years after starting my search I was looking at images of a Victorian sailing ship on the sea floor of the Northwest Passage. HMS *Breadalbane* had three masts, a flat-roofed deck house, and a wide cargo hold. She had been carrying supplies for a British naval expedition in 1853 when she was crushed by the ice, and as her twenty-one crew members scrambled across the ice to the sanctuary of a second ship, *Breadalbane* sank in three hundred feet of water. When we discovered her, she was still upright on her copper-sheathed keel, and her two forward masts were still standing.

There were four of us in the tent staring at the video monitor. A thick bundle of cables snaked across the floor and down through a hole in the ice. I turned to Chris Nicholson, the vehicle's inventor and chief pilot.

"Great job, Chris. Bring her up and we'll send a diver down."

As Nicholson steered the vehicle back to its recovery cage, I slipped into my parka and stepped outside.

The sun glaring off the sea ice made me wince. It was twenty below zero, with frozen white pressure ridges in every direction.

To the north lay the snow-covered cliffs of Beechey Island. Nearby, on a long pan of ice was a makeshift airstrip, where aircraft had flown in tons of equipment from our base in Resolute Bay. A short walk away were the four insulated tents that housed our living quarters and mess hall, and, beyond them, the big tent protecting our two manned diving systems—the "WASPS."

They were called WASPS because of their armoured, insect-like shape. The diver—shielded from the cold and pressure of the Arctic Ocean—looked through an acrylic dome and breathed air from a finely tuned life-support system. Powered by six small thrusters, the WASP allowed the diver to manoeuvre slowly through the depths. To pick up small objects he placed his arms inside two flexible conduits and grasped rotating-grip manipulators.

Suddenly, my head began to spin and my knees buckled. I took a deep breath and leaned against a fuel drum.

I was exhausted. Years of preparation, months of planning, and the stress of leading twenty-three men into one of the most hostile places on the planet had caught up with me. Five hundred miles north of the Arctic Circle, far from the nearest community, we faced heart-stopping cold, roaming polar bears, and winds that might shred the tents. And there was the constant threat that the ice beneath our feet might crack open. There would be no warning. The hard whiteness would split apart and expose a ragged stretch of black water. A tent and its occupants could be gone within seconds.

There were other dangers, too. The night before, we had been blindsided by a fire. It started sometime after midnight, a small orange flame licking up from a crack in the fuel line of the stove in a sleeping tent. Surrounded by duffle bags and boots, eight men were asleep on their cots. The flames spread and began to feed on the kerosene in the stove's drip pan. Ten feet away, outside the tent wall, was a forty-five-gallon fuel drum, like the one I now leaned against.

Mike Cole, an electronics technician from *National Geographic*, was sleeping in the cot next to the stove. He smelled smoke, knelt on the ice-cold floor in the darkness, and found the fire extinguisher. He pulled the pin and squeezed the trigger. The flames fell and seemed to disappear. Men sat up rubbing their eyes. Someone in underwear and boots ran to the next tent to get a second fire extinguisher.

Coughing violently, Cole leaned in to check the base of the stove. A bright flash of flame drove him back so he squeezed the trigger again and held it. A man appeared outside the tent window, wrestling with the fuel line shutoff valve. Barely able to breathe, Cole fired another burst at the base of the stove and saw the flames die. With tears in his eyes, he staggered toward the door and fresh air.

Two men arrived with back-up extinguishers but the fire was out. A man's arm went around Cole's shoulder. Another guided him toward the mess tent. I examined him, made sure he was okay and then we had coffee and a long conversation. At two-twenty in the morning we finally slouched off to sleep.

I tossed and turned for the rest of the night thinking of how lucky we'd been. But it wasn't simply luck. Mike Cole confirmed that the real assets of this expedition were not in its advanced technologies, but in the physical robustness and mental resilience of every participant.

DURING THE previous thirteen years, I'd led nine research expeditions under the ice of the Arctic Ocean. We had dived in the Mackenzie River Delta, off the north coast of Alaska, off Baffin Island, and in the Northwest Passage. On one of our expeditions we constructed the first polar undersea station. On another we made the first science dives under the pack ice at the North Pole. There were days when the sun was below the horizon, the wind-chill was minus

50°, and the ocean was cold enough to kill unprotected divers in minutes. Some eight hundred dives were successful because every participant was disciplined, determined, and tireless.

I was a leader shaped by the lethal physics of the ocean. On oil rigs and work barges in the Gulf of Mexico and the North Sea I had been responsible for the health and safety of industrial divers working at depths of six hundred feet. It was dangerous work and there were accidents. Sometimes men were badly injured by frayed lift-wires, overheated machinery, or the cold and pressure of the depths. Some had broken legs, smashed ribs, and crushed fingers. Others were maimed by decompression sickness, gas embolism, and hypothermia. A few had faces stilled by death.

My *Breadalbane* team had no idea how consumed I was with their safety. After looking into the eyes of young men killed by bubbles in the brain stem or the explosive flames of an oxygen fire, I became focused on the subject to the point of obsession.

IT WOULD be thirty minutes before the WASP diver suited up and made his way down to the wreck so I tightened my parka hood and started walking toward the scene of the fire.

During the previous five years, the iron-hard ice beneath my boots had taught me more than I ever wanted to know about frustration and failure. On our first search expedition for HMS *Breadalbane* we built a shore camp on Beechey Island and spent ten days using two inflatable boats and a sonar-scanning device to probe the ice-choked waters. We towed the sonar through wind-rows of ice, but saw nothing but empty swaths of sea floor. The following year I put a larger team and better technology on a Canadian Coast Guard icebreaker. There was more snow, and the ice was thicker. We steamed back and forth through two blizzards and more ramparts of ice, but saw no evidence of the drowned ship.

One of the things that kept me going was that our primary mission went beyond finding the ship. By working here day after day we were confirming Canadian sovereignty over its northern ocean. We were developing new search and recovery techniques that could be used by the coast guard and navy. With Russian and American nuclear submarines roaming under the ice pack, locating and recovering objects on the sea floor was a critical national asset.

After two search expeditions and six months spent in libraries in Ottawa and Cambridge, England, the project had become part of me. I was one with the *Breadalbane* and her unknown position under the ice. I was beginning to understand the long, freezing spaces inside the Arctic Ocean. Because the forces within the spaces were emergent and unpredictable, I had to have perspective on complex systems; I had to experiment and adapt.

I'd spent hundreds of hours studying nineteenth-century British naval history and felt I knew the officers and crew of HMS *Breadalbane*. They were tough, self-reliant young men who understood the perils of fractured ice and pressure ridges. They had the experience and endurance to venture beyond the edge of the known earth.

I imagined their captain as someone in his early thirties who'd learned his skills on a whaling ship. Determined, disciplined, and competent, he fought his way into the Northwest Passage, watched the polar ice pack surround his vessel, ordered his crew over the side, and led them to safety.

Inspired by the courage of these men, I decided to lead one more search for their ship. I fine-tuned the team and the technology, and we loaded fifty cases of equipment on the coast guard icebreaker *Sir John A. MacDonald*. On the second search day a ghostly outline appeared on the sonar printout. The 184-year-old ship was upright on the sea floor with her bow pointing east.

Within weeks I was making plans to explore her hull and deck house with a remotely operated video camera. I wanted to know the extent of the ice damage and what could be seen through her open deck-house windows.

According to polar experts, April was the best month for the work because it brought long days of sunlight to the Northwest Passage at a time when the pack ice was still solid enough to build a camp over the wreck. However, three weeks prior to the expedition, a reconnaissance flight revealed that the wind-driven ice was shifting and had buckled. Reluctantly I postponed the expedition until the following year.

Twelve months later the polar pack was again grinding itself into vertical blocks and sloping pans. For a second time I called every member of the team to say the expedition was postponed. My voice conveyed a sense of inadequacy and hopelessness. After five years of fighting with the ice I was considering calling it quits.

Something beyond the frustration and failure kept me on course. I had an obligation to my team and the people who'd supported us. I was still learning and adapting. I would give it one more try.

This time the ice was frozen solid—for the moment. We'd made five dives with the videocam robot and three with the WASP. I was slowly realizing that I'd found more than a shipwreck; I had discovered that in the darkest moments your résumé and background mean nothing; the only things that matter are the choices you make and your commitment to them.

No one was inside the sleeping tent so I closed the door behind me, walked between two rows of empty bunks, and bent down to check the stove. The fuel line had been replaced and the stove was on low heat.

I was beyond grateful. My team leaders, including Phil Nuytten who headed the WASP dive team, Emory Kristof who led the

National Geographic photographic team, and Pete Jess who managed camp logistics, had the same qualities as Mike Cole. They'd made sacrifices and had doubts, but consistently came through with flawless performances. They would commit everything—their reputation, their careers, perhaps even their lives—to succeed in the mission.

As I made my way across the ice to the WASP tent, I imagined the diver in the darkness below. The water in front of him was transparent, flowing from a soft blue to a deep navy. The water beneath him was midnight black.

He would be trying to find the ship. His slim communication and power cable ran upward until it disappeared in the shivering water below the WASP tent.

As he descended he would pass one of the masts jutting up like a giant spear. Then he would slow his descent and hover over the forward roof of the deck house looking down on carved railings and fallen spars.

The ship was a great black ghost of a thing, the sweep of her long deck reaching out on all sides. Somewhere overhead, his cable ran between the masts.

His face almost touching the acrylic dome, he would peer into the deck house—a tightly framed space, with benches, tables, and chairs bolted to the deck. A century-old room preserved under the ice. Trying to gauge the strength of the current, he would ease his thrusters forward and head toward the stern.

I walked into the bright lights and diesel roar of the dive tent, stood next to the big hole in the ice, and heard Phil Nuytten shout into his headset, "Doug—where the hell are you?"

Through the static I heard a big man grunting.

Doug Osbourne looked up through his acrylic dome at the tower of water over his head. He was on the starboard side of the ship. On two previous dives he'd landed on the port side, but this time the current forced him across the deck and wrapped his cable around one of the masts.

Osbourne had made thirty-two dives in the WASP suit, most of them to inspect and repair offshore oil platforms. He was in a fix, but no big deal. In the distance were the faint lights of the videocam robot. A second WASP suit with a standby diver was ready to go. He was still warm inside his thick woollen underwear, and there was plenty of time.

As I listened to the sound of his breathing, my heart rate doubled at the thought of what might happen next. The cable might twist and we'd lose voice contact. If we couldn't free him, his body temperature would drop, his coordination and judgment would diminish and we'd have a five-star crisis. If the diesel generator picked this moment for a mechanical breakdown, we'd have a ten-star crisis.

Nuytten was an accomplished WASP pilot who had made the first dive to the ship, and so for both men it was basically a problem of relationships. Was the cable above or below the crosstree? How strong was the current and what direction was it flowing?

"Should we send the videocam over to take a look?" asked Osbourne.

"Negative. Its cable might get hooked around yours."

For the next ten minutes Nuytten used hand signals to choreograph the actions of three men working the cable control and winch drum. They gingerly lifted and lowered the snagged cable. Four men on the ice and the big man in the depths were locked into each other, making it up from past experiences, improvising like a hot jazz group.

"Bring me up slowly and then give me some slack," said Osbourne.

"Bringing you up slowly and giving you some slack."

"Okay. Hold that."

"Roger. All hold."

"I'll try full power on the thrusters."

Seconds ticked by.

"Where are you?"

"Beside the foremast. Cable's clear. It's resting on a windlass."

I stopped hyperventilating and turned away so Nuytten couldn't see the sweat gleaming on my forehead.

"Want us to pull you over to the port side so you can go aft?"

"Negative. I'll stay here for a minute. The forward wall of the deck house is gone and I can see directly into it."

The sweat had run into my eyes and I couldn't see anything. Another save-the-mission performance. Another lethal bullet dodged.

I WAS thirty-three years old when I led my first research team under the ice of the Arctic Ocean. The only things I had going for me were gut instincts and the outstanding performance of my teammates. Thirteen years and ten expeditions later, I was still struggling with the challenge of how to be a good leader.

In truth, I was still sleepwalking through leadership. I had only a vague notion about how real leaders think and act. My guiding principle was to get the best people, give them what they needed, get out of the way, and let them deliver. And they did.

But shortly after my last Arctic expedition, RMS *Titanic* was discovered two and a half miles beneath the North Atlantic. The event drew me toward the men and machines exploring the uttermost depths of the ocean. It was two years later, when I made my first dive to the world's most famous shipwreck, that I became a serious student of leadership. My observations and reading became more systematic and sustained. Then, during a keynote presentation in the Czech Republic, I discovered how much more I still had to learn.

The author and the *Deep Rover* sub team.

SERIOUS STUDENT

"SHE WAS a cylindrical cave of technology—three storeys high, longer than a football field, and powered by the furious heat of her nuclear reactor. She was one thousand feet beneath the Norwegian Sea heading toward her home port near Murmansk."

I was in Prague, giving a speech to five hundred employees and partners of GE Energy. I was standing at centre stage, talking without notes, telling a story that had become a fixation.

"As a research ship and combat sub, the *Komsomolets* was designed to hunt and destroy the ships of the American fleet. She had a unique titanium hull and could dive to a depth of three thousand feet. Everything from her spherical bow to her single, seven-bladed propeller was built to make her invisible to the enemy. The only projection from her smooth, elongated shape was a high, fin-like sail holding a cluster of periscopes and a control station. It was late in the morning and her sixty-nine officers and men were quietly obeying orders issued from the control centre in the middle of the ship."

My lecture agent in London had booked the speech six months earlier. In the conference brochure I was described as the "keynote speaker who will address the delegation with a presentation entitled 'Exploration, Discovery and Leadership: Insights from Deep-Sea Explorers.'" I gave about twenty keynote presentations every year and felt comfortable on the wide, well-lit stage. I knew my subject and had practised my delivery.

"The foremost compartment held ten torpedoes, two with nuclear warheads. The reactor was in a large compartment near the centre of the ship. It was a gigantic, barrel-shaped vessel with thick, reinforced walls. Inside, under a dome of pressurized steam, was a forest of nuclear fuel rods, each as thick as a man's finger. Immersed in water at a temperature of 350 degrees Celsius, the fuel rods shimmered in a pale, blue light."

I scanned the first three rows of the audience. They were men and women whose professional lives were devoted to the development and use of complicated systems. They looked upward, pondering my words.

"The men under Captain Vanin's command operated the most advanced nuclear reactor in the Soviet navy. They had spent years mastering nuclear physics, fluid systems, and reactor engineering. They were a fraternity of perfectionists who spent most of their time thinking about corrosion, containment, and coolant purification.

"Late in the morning a fire broke out in an electrical panel in compartment number seven near the stern. The smoke overwhelmed the seaman standing watch. The heat burst an air pipe and the high-pressure air turned the fire into an inferno. Although trained for an emergency like this, the firefighting teams were unable to contain the flames. Seals and fittings around the propeller shaft melted and seawater burst in, pulling the stern downward. Five hours after the fire started, a bank of high-pressure oxygen cylinders blew up and Captain Vanin ordered his men to abandon ship. Fifty-six men, most of them in sweat-drenched overalls, jumped into the freezing water and scrambled for the life rafts. Thirty minutes later, the giant sub disappeared beneath the surface."

I glanced down at the front row. A young man in a dark blazer was writing on a notepad.

"As the crew struggled to get into the overturned rafts, the huge sub dropped swiftly through the darkness. She landed on the bottom, a mile below the surface, virtually intact, her keel embedded in the sediments. Bubbles streamed out of her broken hull."

During the next few minutes, I told the story of how my Russian colleagues, using their two twenty-million-dollar *Mir* research subs, had surveyed the wreckage and taken photographs and water samples. Water and sediments near the sub were radioactive. Concerned that the military would hide the facts, my colleagues asked me to tell the story of what they had found. The young man was still writing.

After I finished speaking, several members of the audience came up and said how much they enjoyed the connections I made between deep-sea leadership and their work in technology and communications. Dark Blazer waited patiently, and then stepped forward. He had light blond hair and mournful eyes.

"I work as a volunteer for the Bellona environmental foundation in Oslo," he told me. His voice was resonant and steady. "We were formed after the Chernobyl disaster. Today, we focus most of our efforts on northwestern Russia where submarine accidents, radioactive storage sites, and the ocean dumping of nuclear waste are responsible for widespread nuclear pollution."

I suggested we talk for a few minutes and we went downstairs to the hotel coffee shop.

He told me that Russia operated sixty-seven nuclear-powered submarines and a pair of nuclear-powered battle cruisers. In addition, they had fifty-two retired nuclear submarines still equipped with fuel rods. All told, the Russian northern fleet had 270 reactors in service or in storage. The risk to human health and the environment was enormous and growing.

The sense of success I had felt on the stage swiftly ebbed. If what he said was true, the *Komsomolets* was part of a much bigger story. The world's highest concentration of active and derelict nuclear reactors was in Russia's Kola Peninsula, and if safety measures were not put in place there might be a major accident and a release of fissile material. This young man and his associates at the Bellona Foundation were struggling to prevent an undersea Chernobyl.

I told him I was embarrassed to be standing on a stage talking like an authority when I only knew part of the story. He smiled and told me that the Cold War arms race had outpaced the ability of authorities to dispose of decommissioned submarines and their nuclear waste. Tons of radioactive materials were stored in makeshift facilities in dozens of navy yards and bases.

My heart sank. A long stretch of Russian coastline on the Arctic Ocean had radioactive hot spots that put nearby communities at risk from invisible, lethal rays. And I knew nothing about it.

It wasn't the first time I'd felt a combination of dread and personal ignorance. In recent months I'd seen an increasing number of reports and articles about overfishing, clear-cutting, urban sprawl, and the thinning of the polar ice pack. In spite of being a doctor who professed to be concerned about safety, I knew little about the increasing threats to human health throughout the world. I was suffering from a case of severe eco-blindness.

As Dark Blazer drank his third cup of coffee he told me about Aleksandr Nikitin, a former captain in the Russian navy who had contributed to the Bellona Report on nuclear problems within the Russian northern fleet. Nikitin was arrested by the Russian police and charged with treason for revealing state secrets, a crime punishable by ten to fifteen years in prison—or even death. Although innocent, he was denied bail and the case dragged through the courts for years until he was finally set free. "Aleksandr is a man of great courage, honour, and conscience," he told me. "An example of what I aspire to become."

I flew back from Prague thinking about Nikitin and the others like him who look into their consciences and act with resolute courage. They were high-risk explorers probing new realms of responsibility toward the earth. Before we landed, I committed myself to a future of filling in the uncomfortable blank spaces in my mind.

I STARTED reading scientific articles and books on radioactivity. I went to the Bellona Foundation website and ordered their publications; I also devoured Greenpeace's fine work on this subject. Out of a welter of technical facts, I began to form a mental picture of the nuclear legacy that started with the making of the atomic bomb and ran through the decades to the accidents at Three Mile Island and Chernobyl. I started drafting a story about the *Komsomolets* called "Fire in the Ocean."

In an attempt to expand my understanding of leadership and teamwork in the wider world, I began talking to scholars and social activists about other threats to our social and planetary systems. Among them was Thomas Homer-Dixon, professor at the University of Waterloo and author of *The Ingenuity Gap* and *The Upside of Down*. "Stupendous changes are converging simultaneously on our societies," he wrote, "On our leaders and on each one of us—leading many to feel that things are out of control, and we're going to crash. If we try to keep things largely the way they are, our societies will become progressively more complex and rigid and, in turn, progressively less creative and able to cope with sudden crises and shocks." In conversations and e-mails, Homer-Dixon encouraged me to explore the dynamics of these crises and shocks and how we might respond to them.

I devoured "global crisis" books written by James Howard Kunstler, George Monbiot, Tim Flannery, Gwynne Dyer, and Thomas Friedman. In his best-selling *Hot, Flat, and Crowded,* Friedman wrote: "The era we are entering will be one of enormous social, political and economic change—driven in large part from above, from the sky, from Mother Nature. How we address these interwoven global trends will determine a lot about the quality of life on earth in the 21st century. We are not ready for this mission. Right now we don't have the focus and persistence to take on something really big, where the benefits play out over the long term. But I believe that all that could change with the right leadership—local, state and federal."

Slowly I became aware of what I call (with thanks to Margaret Atwood) the thirty-seven "blind assassins." They are summarized each year for the Davos Economic Forum and under the headings Water Scarcity and Drought, Food Shortages and Famine, Poverty and Crashing Economies, International Terrorism and Failed States, National and International Wars, Pandemics and Super-Bugs. The list also includes Risk of Nuclear War and Loose Nukes, Rising Sea Levels and Massive Population Shifts, The End of Cheap Oil and Shifts to Clean Energy, Species Extinction, Global Drug Use, and Cyberwar.

As part of my emerging awareness, I initiated a multimedia project called "Wisdom Keepers: One Generation Speaks to the Next." A series of short interviews with men and women—artists, scientists, politicians, and poets who enhance our understanding of the human family and the natural world—Wisdom Keepers was designed to inspire a sense of enterprise and ingenuity in young people. Jane Goodall, Pete Seeger, Margaret Atwood, Robert Bateman, Jean-Michel Cousteau, Robert

Kennedy Jr. and many others told me stories of leadership challenges overcome and hard-won lessons learned.

Slowly I began to realize that I was responsible for some of the problems and unless I did something to combat them, I was participating in them. After some hard thinking I decided to write a book about leadership in high-risk environments and how studying its components and taking specific steps can make us better leaders.

For the purposes of this book, leadership in high-risk environments—*deep leadership*—is the ability to make critical team decisions to accomplish challenging missions in the abyssal ocean, in outer space, and on the battlefield. Deep leadership is radically different than political and business leadership. Make a leadership mistake working four thousand metres beneath the ocean, on the International Space Station or a military base in Afghanistan and you can lose more than money or jobs. You can lose lives—including your own. That's why I call it *deep leadership*. That's why it's such a compelling model to help us understand and develop our own leadership traits.

IN THE next section I'll introduce you to some of the individuals and events that have informed me about the essential traits of deep leadership. Some occurred early in my career; some took place recently. I've selected each story because of its lasting impact on my thinking.

PART TWO:

ESSENTIAL TRAITS OF LEADERSHIP

The 'Original 7' Mercury astronauts.

COOL COMPETENCE
MASTERY OF SPECIFIC SKILLS TO EXCEL IN HIGH-RISK CONDITIONS

THE MAN running next to me was five-feet-nine inches tall, weighed a hundred and fifty-five pounds, and had the perfect frame to squeeze into a small spacecraft.

"Pick up the pace, guys," he said. "Pick up the pace."

In 1962, a tiny space capsule atop a Mercury-Atlas rocket had carried Scott Carpenter up to an altitude of 164 miles and an orbital velocity of 17,532 miles per hour. For the next five hours he circled the planet three times, performed precision manoeuvres with his spacecraft, took photographs, made observations, and carried out five experiments. He was the second American to orbit the earth. Carpenter had slender shoulders, muscular arms, and the military habit of speaking slowly to make sure his words were clear.

Now he was running easily by my side. I tried to run harder. Sweat flew off my fingertips.

On that scorcher of a morning there were forty-five of us jogging on an asphalt roadway past the grey seawalls and warships of the San Francisco Naval Shipyard. My lungs were on fire and my heart was pounding. I started to fall back. Carpenter turned and gave me *that look.* I put my head down and leaned into it, moving my legs faster.

Carpenter and the men beside me radiated animal vitality. They had been chosen for this navy project because of their competence, devotion to duty, and unquestioning belief in the mission. I was carried forward by the strength of their stride and the fierceness of their will.

SHORTLY AFTER his historic flight, Carpenter had retired from NASA to focus his attention on research that would allow navy divers to live in undersea stations. As a team leader in Sealab II he spent thirty days living at 205 feet. His engineering intelligence and high-risk experience made him the ideal deputy on-scene commander for Sealab III, a ten-million-dollar project designed to allow teams of military and civilian divers to live for weeks beneath the Pacific Ocean off the California coast.

Needing additional medical support for the project, the navy contracted Ocean Systems for my services. Three months before the launch of Sealab III, I moved to San Francisco and began training with the divers under Carpenter's command.

In San Francisco, Carpenter and I became friends. We were part of a team that started each day with arm-burning calisthenics and a two-mile run, and then spent the next ten hours listening to lectures from naval experts, or diving with our new breathing rigs in the grim, twilight waters of the bay. I saw the look of pain on his face when Sealab was lowered to a depth of six hundred feet and Barry Cannon, one of the best divers on the team, was killed trying to open its main hatch.

Severely stressed from overwork and hypothermia, and using a technically inadequate breathing system, Cannon had suffered a fatal seizure.

At the University of Colorado, Carpenter worked on a degree in aeronautical engineering. He joined the navy, became a pilot, and flew multi-engine patrol planes. At the Navy Test Pilot School he flew every operational and experimental airplane in the fleet. Recognizing his ability with electronics, navigation, and communications, NASA selected him for its first team of astronauts. "They wanted flight-proven pilots," he told me, "With a wide range of skills."

During their first year of training, the seven Project Mercury astronauts studied astronomy, physics, aeronautics, and physiology. They pored over stacks of technical literature on their spacecraft and its launch, flight, and re-entry procedures. They practised coping with life-threatening hazards including an explosion of their spacecraft's launch escape system.

I asked Carpenter how he handled the uncertainty and risks.

"We were trained to avoid active intellectual comprehension of danger and disaster. We were too busy learning how to perform our tasks. When you're in a high-risk profession, you learn to park your emotions.

"What perils did we face? The retrorockets might explode. They might not burn properly. The heat shield might fail. The drogue or the main chute might not deploy. If you thought about all the things that could go wrong, you'd never climb into a spacecraft. You count on all those things going right because you've got confidence in the systems, the men and women on the ground, and yourself."

CARPENTER'S MERCURY spacecraft had ten thousand parts and held one person. Within arm's reach were fifty-five electrical switches, thirty fuses, and thirty-five mechanical levers. As his friend John Glenn said, "We didn't ride the Mercury capsule, we wore it."

Just before Carpenter re-entered the atmosphere, his pitch horizon scanner intermittently malfunctioned. He took over manual control. "The last thirty minutes of my flight were dicey. The retrorockets were supposed to fire automatically. I watched the second hand pass the mark, and when they didn't fire, I punched the retro-button. An agonizing three seconds passed until the sound of retro-rockets filled the cabin. My visual reference was divided between the periscope, the window, and the attitude indicators. Looking out the window helped me maintain the desired pitch of 34 degrees."

In spite of his efforts, the scanner malfunction and loss of thrust in the retrorockets produced an overshoot of 250 miles. For forty minutes the world held its breath wondering whether he'd landed safely.

Finally, Carpenter and his capsule were lifted out of the Atlantic and placed on the deck of the aircraft carrier USS *Intrepid*. Flight data analysis confirmed that the pilot's calibrated proficiency saved the mission.

"COMPETENCE IS the heart of it," she said. "You need intimate knowledge of every step in the mission. Competence is the cornerstone."

Julie Payette was sitting in her office at the Manned Space Center in Houston talking to me on the phone two weeks before the space shuttle carried her and six crewmates up to an altitude of 256 miles, an orbital velocity of 17,532 miles per hour, and a rendezvous with the International Space Station. She spoke quickly with the tempo of someone who didn't waste time.

Payette was an extremely handsome forty-five-year-old woman with serious brown eyes and red-blond hair that spilled over her shoulders. When she smiled the edge of her mouth hinted of the mischievous girl within. Lithe and muscular, she gave the impression she could arm-wrestle anyone in the room.

Payette had a bachelor of engineering degree from McGill University and a master's of applied science in electrical and computer engineering from the University of Toronto. She'd worked as a systems engineer and visiting scientist for IBM in Canada and Switzerland. "Engineering teaches you how to look at a problem," she told me, "To analyze it, see what resources are available, and solve it. It's essentially what we do in space."

In 1999, Payette flew her first mission on board the shuttle *Discovery*. The crew performed the first manual docking to the space station and delivered four tons of supplies. Payette supervised an eight-hour spacewalk to repair the station, operated the Canadarm, and monitored the station life-support and engineering systems.

During her upcoming mission, she was the flight engineer sitting between the commander and pilot in what she called "the best seat in the house." In front of her were five windows, dozens of controls and switches, an abort panel, five identical IBM general-purpose computers, and eleven full-colour flat-panel displays. With more than ten million parts, *Endeavour* was the most complex machine ever built.

I asked her about the versatility needed to be a shuttle astronaut. "Exploring every frontier from mountains to oceans was done by people in small groups," she said. "Success depended upon everyone's ability to do many tasks. If each person has only one job and someone is incapacitated, the mission is compromised. In space, we do everything. We're the cleaner, the cook, the robotics operator, the proxy scientist, and the space walker."

During her sixteen-day mission Payette assisted the commander and pilot in docking with the space station. During the six-and-a-half-million-mile flight, she operated three different robotic arms for five spacewalks. She worked with the crew to complete the construction of the Kibo Japanese Experiment Module, deliver spare parts and replacement batteries, and install scientific experiments.

Although their flights into space were almost a half-century apart, Carpenter and Payette personify the cool competence mantra: practise, practise, practise. One of their top priorities—realistic, demanding training—allowed them to perform critical tasks flawlessly under pressure.

THE GREATEST gift of individuals like Carpenter and Payette may not be in how they perform as they orbit the earth at 17,532 miles an hour, but how they give wings to the aspirations of the rest of us. I remember the electric thoughts running through my mind when John Glenn and Scott Carpenter were looking down at the world from their perilous perches in the heavens. I can't be an astronaut, I said to myself; it is a career far beyond my reach. But I can try to understand the attributes that go into the making of an astronaut. If I'm really observant and persistent, perhaps I can come up with my own version of those attributes. It's a task I've been pursuing ever since.

REFLECTIONS ON COOL COMPETENCE

If you don't rehearse over and over, you're going to be surprised in space. And the surprised man out there is the dead man. We get ready, then, by trying to surprise ourselves.
—RICHARD F. GORDON JR.,
GEMINI AND APOLLO ASTRONAUT

LEADERSHIP IS not about a rigid set of rules and standards; it's about relationships, it's about the complex ways people influence, inform, and inspire each other.

COOL COMPETENCE—mastering specific skills to overcome uncertain conditions—is an essential trait of leadership. It infuses and makes possible all the other traits including fierce ingenuity and blood trust.

In his book about the original seven Mercury astronauts, Tom Wolfe coined the phrase "the right stuff." A special version of cool competence, he describes "the right stuff" as when one has "the ability to go up in a hurtling piece of machinery to the outer edge of the sky and has the moxie, the experience, the coolness to pull it back at the last yawning moment—and repeat this thick adrenalin moment the next day—and the next."

One of the curses of competence is the intoxication of pure expertise. After gaining mastery of one field we're tempted to say, "I'm good at this; I must be good at that." A second curse is to confuse expertise with leadership. Expertise is only one component. The mother curse is the one that can bring you to your knees in an instant—overconfidence.

Central to Julie Payette's notion of competence is teamwork. "When you're an astronaut being a team player is your whole life," she told me. "Cohesiveness is so important. Being glued together allows us to quickly sense change and adapt to it." She also believes that leadership and teamwork traits are interchangeable. Like her crewmates, she's mastered the subtle choreography of leading and following at the same time.

Systems are simple and predictable or complex and dynamic. A booster rocket is a simple system. An astronaut team is a complex system. In every system, the function of the parts is studied and synthesized into the performance of the whole. Leaders learn that analysis begins by *looking into the parts* and synthesis begins by *looking out from the parts*. While they're working on one of the parts, they never lose sight of the system and the bigger systems that contain it.

"Astronauts work in an interconnected, uncertain environment," Carpenter told me. "You learn about electrical systems, mechanical systems, biological systems, and team systems. You're on intimate terms with feedback loops and systems embedded within systems. To perform effectively you develop systems thinking."

Scott Carpenter grounded his technical skills in his physical toughness. When the NASA doctors put him on a treadmill or tested his breath-holding capacity he broke their physiological records. After two hours at a simulated low-oxygen altitude of 65,000 feet, his pulse rate and blood pressure remained rock steady. "You can do anything if you're motivated," he told me. "And I was motivated."

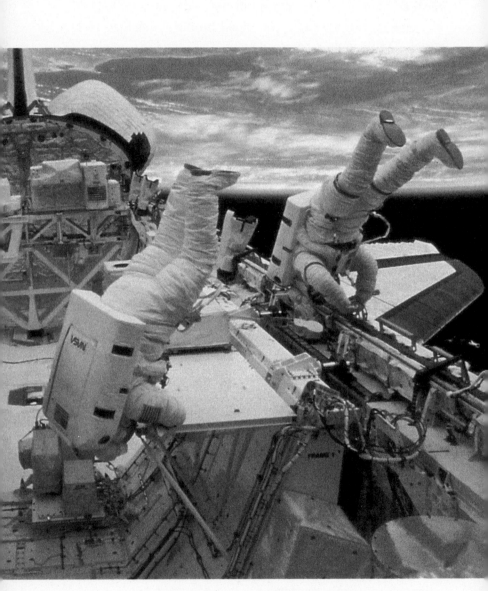

Kathy Sullivan making a spacewalk.

POWERFUL
PRESENTATIONS
MASTERY OF WRITTEN AND SPOKEN WORDS THAT COMMAND THE MOMENT

"YOU HAVE to learn how to express yourself. You have to learn how to convey the idea you have and what it could mean and where you might take it. You can signal a lot of that stuff through short e-mails or very brief answers, but at some point, to bring people with you—you have to tell the whole story. And you have to watch people and see that your words and metaphors are clicking with them. Do they get it? Are they feeling the same thing you're feeling? There are deep human roots of caring, compassion, security, fear, and need. The vibrant power of communication is to use words to tap into those roots."

I was listening to Kathy Sullivan, the first American woman to walk in space, a scientist-astronaut who'd flown three shuttle missions and spent more than five hundred hours orbiting the planet.

We were in Washington DC, participating in the Sea Space Symposium founded by a small group of former astronauts, navy officers, government officials, and business leaders who met annually to discuss scientific issues in the ocean and in space. This year's topics included the technical challenges of a Mars mission and the multiple impacts of climate change. On this warm

October night, one of our members had arranged a dinner in the Mansfield Room in the Senate Wing of the Capitol Building.

The dinner was over and Sullivan was standing in front of a white marble fireplace flanked by the American and US Senate flags. On the walnut-panelled wall behind her hung a life-sized painting of Senator Mike Mansfield in a dark blue suit with his hands folded across his chest. The longest-serving majority leader in the Senate, Mansfield was an ardent supporter of President Kennedy. During his thirty-four years in Congress he introduced the Civil Rights Act of 1964 and asked hard questions about US involvement in Vietnam. After leaving the Senate, he served two presidents as the American ambassador to Japan.

Kathy Sullivan was the kind of person who belonged in a historic room like this. Three years after the shuttle's first flight, she and Dave Leestma floated out of its mid-deck airlock in their spacesuits to test a set of specialized tools designed to refill satellite propellant tanks. At one point during the three-and-a-half-hour EVA, Sullivan glanced down at her feet. "I had the entire coast of Venezuela sliding beneath my boots at 17,532 miles an hour."

Twenty-five years after her historic spacewalk, Sullivan was the director of mathematics and science education policy at the Battelle Center at Ohio State University. Earlier that day, between sessions, I asked her to describe herself.

"I'm a scientist, astronaut, and explorer. The scientist observes closely, asks questions, teases things apart, tries to understand them and build answers that can help do something about them. The astronaut has a perspective from orbiting around the earth, a perspective about myself and people and teamwork and the challenges that come from mastering the task of putting together a space mission and flying it successfully. First and foremost I'm an explorer because as a young girl I was curious about everything. I read books ravenously. I love having the chance to wonder and probe and experience things. Exploration gives me a richer sense of who I am and the world around me."

Speaking on a stage to a thousand people or talking to you personally in a crowded room, Sullivan had the gift of all great speakers. She articulated in fine, short phrases, knew every dimension of her subject, and always seemed to find the right balance between detail and emotion. She knew the real secret of powerful presentations was authenticity, the ability to be genuine and speak from her heart. When she expressed the spirit of scientific exploration and discovery, she made you feel you were part of something big and important.

Sullivan was fifty-eight years old, but looked much younger. She had honey-brunette hair, bright hazel-green eyes, a PhD in geology, and a lifelong passion for science and engineering. During her second mission, her crew released the Hubble Space telescope into orbit 350 miles above the earth. During the release, Sullivan and Bruce McCandless were suited up in the airlock ready to exit if the telescope's solar arrays needed unfolding.

"Hubble is my proudest professional accomplishment at NASA," she wrote afterward. "And I don't just mean the 1990 flight when we deployed it. I spent a lot of time underwater in the big pool practising spacewalks, helping to verify tasks for the later repair missions. Where does the spacewalking astronaut need to stand? What's the best angle to approach it from? Every time a servicing mission goes up and does five spacewalks' worth of magic to keep this incredible telescope working, I join the ranks of the thousands of nameless people who stood behind me on my flights. My fingerprints are all over the repair crews' success, but I've got even more respect for the people who make shuttle flights happen."

Two years later, Sullivan flew her third and final mission. Her cool-headedness and commitment did not go unnoticed. She was awarded the NASA Exceptional Service Medal, the NASA Medal for Outstanding Leadership and was inducted into the Astronaut Hall of Fame.

"What's the most essential leadership trait?" I asked.

"There are two critical traits: perspective and composure. To be a leader, you have to have perspective. You have to be able to see further, walk ahead, and draw people with you. You need composure because when you lead people into difficult things, even really cool stuff, there are hard and frightening moments. When you encounter them, you need a clearer vision, a steadier hand, and a calmer gaze. You connect your perspective and composure with your team in a way that encourages them to move forward—even when their instinct says 'We don't know if we can do this.'

"That's leading. Sometimes you have to do it with yourself and for yourself. Sometimes you're more outward focused and do it for other people. My first small steps in leadership meant developing perspective and composure for myself about something that flustered or frightened me. I found I could pause, observe, and reflect. I could shift gears on a small challenge and figure a way past it. It meant the next challenge could be a little bigger. And the next one even bigger.

"That's how leadership starts. It starts with you. You make a commitment to leadership. You learn how to write—really well—and build a library of books and experiences. You develop confidence in your ability to orient yourself and make sense of the things that shock you. Then you develop the ability to connect your perspective and composure with other people.

"That's why communication is such a critical leadership ingredient. The success of each mission and the hard, repetitive tasks within each mission, means finding the right words to convey your vision to your teammates."

Sullivan—astronaut, chief scientist of the National Oceanic and Atmospheric Administration, presidential appointee to the National Science Board—was a deep leader wherever she went. She was very persuasive and a shrewd negotiator. She had the capacity to look at herself from the outside, assess what she was doing, and take steps to improve herself. She was dedicated to a life of service: to her crewmates, to science, to her country.

I HAVE a confession to make. I have a crush on Kathy Sullivan. It's the authenticity thing. The first American woman to walk in space hasn't an ounce of pretension in her. I've dived with her under the ocean and watched her speak her quicksilver-reasoning mind in small groups and large. In everything she does, what you see is what you get. When I'm in her company, which is not often enough, I'm reminded how much work I have to do to shore up the weaknesses in my leadership traits.

REFLECTIONS ON POWERFUL PRESENTATIONS

MY FIRST major keynote presentation was at an IBM Golden Circle in Singapore. We'd just discovered the world's northernmost known shipwreck HMS *Breadalbane* and I was asked to give a sixty-minute speech about our three-year search. The IBM event coordinator gave me blue-ribbon advice. "You're going to stand up in front of five hundred people and you're going to be nervous. There's only one way to fly your butterflies in formation. Prepare and practise. Tell a story. Be funny. Be humble."

Since then I've given presentations to more than one hundred IBM audiences in North America, Europe, and the Far East. I've spoken to Fortune 500 audiences including Microsoft, General Motors, Toshiba, Fidelity, and Toyota and given speeches at the Smithsonian Institution, National Geographic, and the US Naval Academy in Annapolis. Here are some of the things I've learned along the way.

Great leaders are great speakers. Barack Obama inspired millions of supporters with his charismatic presence, rousing rhetoric, and hope for the future. Obama's "hope" is the same as that described by Vaclav Havel, playwright, human rights activist, and former president of the Czech Republic: "Hope is the certainty that something makes sense, regardless of how it turns out." Obama knew from the beginning of his professional life that if he was to succeed he had to master the art of persuasion and the power of presentation. Over the years he honed his written and spoken techniques of conveying vision, earning trust, and motivating others.

THERE ARE three kinds of speakers: informational speakers, entertaining speakers, and motivational speakers. Informational speakers are good at getting information across. They have PowerPoint slides with charts and graphs. (Think Al Gore talking about *An Inconvenient Truth*.) They don't tell stories, and they frequently repeat the information on their slides. Entertaining speakers have a lot of energy and an amusing delivery that keeps listeners interested in what they're saying. (Think Jerry Seinfeld hosting the Oscars.) Their presentation is a nice experience, but leads to nothing of consequence. Motivational speakers are a combination of informational and entertaining speakers. They're passionate about their subject. They share information in a provocative way that leads to action. (Think Martin Luther King.) They inspire their audiences to want to do something about what they've just heard.

Leadership is words and images. Any presentation, from a tweet to a keynote, is measured by how effectively we use sentences and "photographic" images—and how well they are converted into positive, meaningful action.

Great public speakers speak without notes, are masters of eye contact, body language, and voice intonation. (Think Bill Clinton talking about his foundation.) As author and communication coach Richard Greene emphasizes, "Great speakers know that rhythm is one of the most important ways to carry and generate emotion." They know the expectations of their audience, how to personalize the message, and make the "we" connection. *Practise* is their middle name. They illustrate their speeches with anecdotes and dynamic images. They close with a crescendo and leave a lasting impression.

Powerful presentations start with powerful writing. Give your letters, text messages, and memos an inner logic, a narrative chronological structure that makes them easy to remember. Be self-deprecating. Open strong. Close stronger.

Special Forces soldier in training.

PHYSICAL ROBUSTNESS
MASTERY OF STRENGTH AND STAMINA TO COMBAT STRESS

FIVE YEARS after the loss of the *Thresher*, I was on a United States Navy ship a few miles south of the island of Terceira in the Azores. We were part of a small fleet searching the eastern Atlantic for the USS *Scorpion*, a fast attack nuclear submarine that had disappeared ten days earlier. Slightly longer than *Thresher*, *Scorpion* had a speed of thirty knots and carried ninety-nine sailors and officers.

Ocean Systems was the prime contractor for the USN's Supervisor of Salvage. Two years earlier we worked with the navy to coordinate the search for the H-bomb that had fallen into the sea when two military aircraft collided over the east coast of Spain. After a three-month search, the bomb was recovered from three thousand feet of water. Forty-eight hours after *Scorpion* was reported missing, the navy loaded our small research sub and six man crew into a CF A and flew us to the Azores to assist in the search.

Called *Deep Diver*, our sub was twenty-two feet long, weighed eight tons, and carried a pilot, copilot, and two divers. A few months earlier, inside the forward chamber, I supervised a "lock-out" dive at seven hundred feet. We found a flat spot on the sea floor and parked the sub. The divers closed off their small steel chamber, suited up, increased the pressure, and swam out through a lower hatch. It was the deepest lock-out dive ever made. If *Scorpion* were found on top of a seamount, four of us would go down in the sub to assess the next step.

During the search the crew on our US Navy ship voiced their respect for men serving on nuclear submarines. "The 'dolphin brotherhood' are the best in the world," they told us. "They train for years. They practise emergency procedures. They don't panic."

Ray Nelson was the crusty, coarse-tongued Chief of the Boat. A single flash of his teeth expressed gratitude, optimism, and anger, all within seconds. He was always in a hurry, striding across the deck on thick-muscled legs.

Chief Nelson bridged the gap between commissioned officers and enlisted men. He relayed the concerns of the crew to the officers, enforced discipline, and smoothed ruffled egos. He was the spine of the ship and had strength of character and human perceptiveness that couldn't be taught. "I've got friends serving on 'nukes'," he told me. "They go through years of rigorous physical and mental training. They know the actions of one man mean life or death for the entire crew. They know that in a crisis you need physical robustness to conduct damage control. You can't abandon ship. No way in hell you're gonna push all that water off you."

After scanning the depths for two weeks, the navy wound down the first phase of the *Scorpion* search. Eight months later, her remains were located at a depth of 10,200 feet. A board of inquiry concluded that a "hot-running" torpedo had detonated inside her pressure hull. Mercifully for the men on board, her end came with devastating quickness.

A FEW years ago, I was invited to deliver the Bock Memorial Lecture at the US Naval Academy in Annapolis. I spent two days looking at the historic parade grounds, athletic fields, and buildings. I saw the darkened crypt where John Paul Jones was buried and the charred space capsule flown by the Mercury astronaut Pete Conrad. The grounds and buildings were breathtaking, but what really impressed me was the raw physical vitality of the midshipmen.

The day after my presentation in Rickover Hall, I spoke to Professor Lew Nuchols about the Academy's physical conditioning program. "We train their bodies as well as their brains," he told me. "We want them faster, stronger, and better in whatever they do. They pick a sport, find a program, and set their own goals. They concentrate on aerobic exercises and strength training. We make sure they've got the right equipment and monitor their progress. The only thing they're short of is sleep."

NOT LONG ago, I flew to Ushuaia, a small town at the southern tip of South America, and boarded a four-hundred-foot Russian icebreaker. It had a Russian crew, a small staff of polar experts, and a hundred passengers, most of us going to the Antarctic for the first time.

Among the passengers were forty physicians attending a symposium on "Medicine in the Extremes." I was a guest lecturer; others included the former head of polar medicine of the Australian Antarctic program and the chief medical officer of NASA.

We spent two days steaming across the six-hundred-mile Drake Passage, a bleak reach of water with a reputation for high winds and two-storey waves. Our destination was the Antarctic Peninsula, a long, north-curving arm of the ice-covered continent.

One night as we headed toward Deception Island, I stood at the bow of the ship looking into the darkness and trying to imagine the men who defined the golden age of Antarctic exploration. Scott, Amundsen, and Shackleton had Edwardian beards and Edwardian attitudes and it was easy to picture them moving across the dreary, white wastes, man-hauling their sledges in temperatures so cold that their breath crystallized and fell to the snow in showers.

Ernest Shackleton's epic voyage in 1916 had haunted me since I was a boy and now I was moving across freezing waters close to where it took place.

Shackleton and his twenty-seven men had almost reached the continent when the ice trapped their two-masted ship for ten months. After it sank, they made camp, drifted on an ice floe for five more months and finally reached a small, uninhabited island. To get help for his men, Shackleton and four others climbed into a small open boat and sailed eight hundred miles to the island of South Georgia.

A swell bigger than the rest rose out of the darkness, lifting our ship, and I could imagine five men wearing filthy clothing, peering out from an old black-and-white photo. They had beards white with frost and were in a twelve-foot wooden boat that looked like it was about to founder. One man, half frozen and half asleep, was at the helm steering east-northeast toward an island he could not see.

After stumbling ashore, Shackleton and his men struggled up a mountain and down to the whaling station on the other coast. They organized a rescue mission, went back for the rest of the crew, and brought everyone home.

REFLECTIONS ON PHYSICAL ROBUSTNESS

THE FIRST thing you notice in every deep leader is enthusiasm—a vital inner strength—for what is being done at the moment. The source of that energy is physical and mental conditioning. *Physical robustness*, the mastery of strength and stamina to combat stress, gives you a positive self-image. It brings vitality to every other trait from cool competence to hot-zone humour.

Physical training is to the military what prayer is to a monastery—an opportunity to build cohesion, deepen obedience, and succeed in the mission.

Before I went to Afghanistan to learn more about warrior leadership, I spent time studying the dynamics of special operations forces in the United States and Canada. "Special forces" are elite military tactical teams trained to perform high-risk missions beyond the reach of conventional troops. Members of these teams are in superb physical condition and have the cool competence and resolute courage to operate individually or in small teams in extremely hostile environments. As Major General Mike Day, leader of Canada's Special Operations Forces Command, told me. "Physical robustness allows you to carry on without having to devote your mental energies to keeping your body going. That's why we're fit. As well, it gives you robustness of spirit—the mental durability to wake up every morning and work ten, twelve, fourteen hours, day in and day out."

The president of the United States gets up most mornings and has a pre-dawn workout. He slips into a tracksuit and ball cap, walks down into the White House gym, and begins exercising with weights and cardio. For him, physical robustness is the engine of his cool competence, powerful presentations, and mental resilience.

Endurance—a sustained form of physical and mental toughness—comes from a bone-deep belief in the mission. But great leaders know their limits. On an earlier expedition to Antarctica, Shackleton had tried to reach the South Pole. A hundred miles short of his goal, he looked at his hungry and exhausted men and decided to turn back. "We look south," he wrote. "We stay only a few moments. Whatever regrets we may have, we have done our best."

Great leaders search for "flow," those moments of heightened awareness when physical toughness and cool competence come together to surmount a specific challenge.

All the advice I've had on physical robustness can be boiled down to this: Exercise six days a week. Do serious aerobic exercise four days a week. Get enough sleep. Don't smoke. Don't eat junk food. Dance carefully with mood-altering drugs like alcohol and caffeine.

No matter how busy they are, leaders find time to exercise. They run, swim, do push-ups, stretch, and eat the right food. They know that leadership is an Olympic event; world-class leaders must be well-trained athletes.

Sustained systemic training is the ultimate performance enhancer; it intensifies your heart's ability to pump blood and your tissues' capacity to use the blood it receives. Exercise changes the structure of the brain and affects thinking. Scientists at the Salk Institute have shown that aerobic exercise—running, cycling, or swimming—stimulates the creation of new brain cells.

Go out hard; when it hurts, keep moving. Pain is just weakness waving goodbye to your body.

Body language always speaks the truth. The way you walk, talk, and hold yourself can't be hidden.

Dr. George Bond (right) and Jacques Cousteau.

HOT-ZONE HUMOUR
MASTERY OF LEVITY AND LAUGHTER TO REDUCE CODE-RED TENSION

I WAS alone in the diving locker back at the US Navy Shipyard in San Francisco, trying to understand the intricacies of the Mark Eight diving helmet, when a powerful voice boomed out behind me.

"Good afternoon, diving doctor."

Captain George Bond's words were deep and resonant, like an old motorcycle warming up. I turned to face him. A pipe with brightly glowing ashes hung from his lower lip.

"How many of your body's two thousand moving parts are in pain today?"

"All of them, sir."

"Does this mean that civilians can't take the navy's physical training?"

"It does, sir. Civilians are used to feather beds and caviar. We are unaccustomed to breaking into a sweat before noon."

Bond was six-foot-three and had extravagant eyebrows, a thatch of white hair and steel-blue eyes. A senior medical officer, he was the driving force behind the navy's Sealab I, II, and III projects. These undersea stations were placed at depths of 193, 215, and 600 feet, and inhabited by teams of navy divers exploring the physical and mental limits of living under the sea. The "father of saturation diving" was a funny, shrewd, and seductive force of nature. First and foremost he was a medical practitioner who listened closely to his men and advised them on their most personal problems. In return they respected him, even loved him. To a man, they called him "Papa Topside."

Bond had hired me to assist him with the medical support of Sealab III. He knew I was having a hard time fitting in to the culture of his hardcore navy divers. Each time we met he tried to ease my uncertainty and bolster my confidence.

"And what are you learning in your work with the navy?" he asked.

"It has given me the desire to be a great doctor, not a great athlete. I'm turning down my offer to play fullback for the Green Bay Packers."

"Wise decision. Two minutes on a football field and your soft pink body would be face up on a stretcher."

SIX MONTHS before, Dr. Bond had asked me to meet him in Washington. When I entered his office at the experimental diving unit, he closed the door and motioned me to sit in a hardbacked chair. He remained standing, his burly frame blocking the light from the window.

"Have you any idea why I've asked you to come here?"

One of Bond's associates had tipped me off about his trenchant humour so I smiled and said softly, "To impart some good news—or bad news, sir."

"The bad news is that you went to the wrong medical school."

"I know, sir. I went to the University of Toronto when I should have attended McGill, the outstanding institution you graduated from."

"I will note the fact that you recognize the difference. The good news is that the navy has approved your consulting contract."

I'd been waiting almost a year for this. Bond and his colleagues were planning to place a station on the Pacific sea floor at 600 feet. It would be occupied for weeks at a time by nine-man teams of aquanauts. I would be working on America's premier sea-floor colony with America's premier diving physician.

"To better understand the physiological and psychological stresses on our men, I want you to train with them. You'll get into shape with them, attend their classes and dive with their equipment. If you qualify, we might put you on one of the teams."

GEORGE BOND grew up in Bat Cave, North Carolina, a settlement of 170 souls near the Great Smoky Mountains. As a young man, he listened to legends and folk songs in remote cabins and shacks and started thinking about the structure and history of language. At the University of Florida at Gainesville, he received a master's degree in English literature. After graduating from medicine at McGill, he spent ten years driving his battered Jeep to places like Turkey Knob and Mountain Home to attend to the medical needs of six thousand people living in the hills and hollows.

Bond's homespun humour came from his native intellect, love of literature, and deep empathy for his hard-working men. In his personal journal (published as *The Sealab Chronicles*) he wrote: "My aquanauts, including Scott Carpenter, are truly a breed apart. They are immensely resourceful, incessantly curious, impervious to hazard and impatient with the progress of the world. They seek the satisfaction of battling odds and attacking new frontiers. A vital ingredient of our success in such hazardous programs is a high degree of loyalty and trust."

As a navy scientist, Bond lived through numerous life-threatening moments. Early in his career, he convinced his superiors to allow him to study the medical effects of making free ascents from disabled submarines. In one test, he donned a buoyant ascent life jacket and swam out of the submarine *Archerfish* in more than 300 feet of water. Kicking hard and exhaling furiously, he and Cyril Tuckfield ascended the height of a thirty-storey building. Their daring, first-ever demonstration set the standard for future submarine escapes.

ON THAT warm September day when we were alone in the Sealab diving locker, Bond looked around the room that housed the helmets, hoses, and hot water suits of his aquanauts. His brow was furrowed from fighting recent bureaucratic brushfires and mechanical problems that had plagued Sealab III for months. He was deeply concerned that another postponement would harm the morale of his men.

More than anyone, Bond knew what navy divers could and could not do with their bodies and their brains. He respected their individualism and cohesiveness. He knew how and when to push them to their limits. He was bold, but when his men were stressed or threatened, he was as cautious as a grandmother.

"And just what do you think of the helmet you are holding in your smooth, unwrinkled, civilian hands?" he asked.

"Well, sir, it worked fine in yesterday's pool dive and I'm sure it will perform well during tomorrow's dive in that miserable corner of the Pacific Ocean known as San Francisco Bay." I held up the heavy fibreglass helmet and peered into its glass faceplate. "But, as you can see, it's as ugly as homemade sin."

Bond took the pipe from his mouth and smiled. "It seems that you have learned one thing well."

"What's that, sir?"

"One of the most important things in a navy diver's tool box is a rustproof sense of humour."

For me, "Papa Topside" was one of those once-in-a-lifetime

mentors. He intuited my feelings and thoughts and responded to my unspoken emotional needs. He made me feel valued and respected. "Papa Topside" gave me much more than advice on diving physiology and psychology; he gave me reassurance. At a critical point in my emerging professional life, he was an emotional refuelling station.

REFLECTIONS ON HOT-ZONE HUMOUR

GREAT LEADERS are levity makers. They can find the humour in anything, especially the urgent and life-and-death stuff. If you can't do that, according to author Laurence Gonzales, "you are already in a world of hurt." Great leaders are always ready with a wry smile, quick wit, and self-deprecating humour. They know that being lighthearted gives the moment a luminous bounce. For them, levity is more about fun than being funny.

Hot-zone humour—using levity and laughter to reduce code-red tension—is an essential trait of leadership. It overlaps with and infuses all other traits, including mental resilience and high-empathy communication. Ingredients of leadership like cool competence and hot-zone humour cannot be taught in books or the classroom; they must be learned by time and events, mistakes and failures. They are shaped by the challenges accepted and self-knowledge achieved.

Deep leaders take their work seriously, themselves not at all. Here's George Bond describing a high-stress moment: "On a bright afternoon, we lowered Sealab II into position southeast of Scripps Canyon before the eyes, ears and cameras of a large assortment of newspaper and TV reporters, who marvelled at the skill of our riggers and the measured cadence of our profanity. For the latter, I offered the excuse that we were carried away or that various pieces of gear were about to be. Today, the image of kindly, lovable, pipe-puffing Papa Topside was replaced by the reality of a ragged, dirty, foul-mouthed old bully."

Humour is not just entertainment. It's a sophisticated form of intelligence that brings confidence and cohesion to the group.

Laughter is a social activity that increases empathy. People who laugh together work well together.

Laughter was an important component in the evolution of highly social humans. In a recent article in the *New York Times*, Robin Dunbar, an evolutionary psychologist at Oxford, suggests that relaxed and contagious social laughter enhances group bonding. Part of the reason for this is the physical act of laughing—*ha, ha, ha*—triggers an increase in endorphins, the brain chemicals known for their feel-good effect.

"Humor represents one of the highest forms of human intelligence," says Daniel Pink in his groundbreaking book *A Whole New Mind*. "Humor embodies the ability to place situations in context, to glimpse the big picture and to combine different perspectives into new alignments."

When adversity struck Bond's undersea missions he focused on his emergency plans. When adversity took a swipe at his teams, he offered his friendship and wit. He knew that the main thing is to focus on the main thing. And the main thing is to accomplish the mission. Being a leader means making tough decisions. Inevitably, some of them will infuriate people. "Making people mad comes with leadership," Bond told me. "You can't please everyone. But hurt feelings cannot compromise the mission. Disarm the anger with discreet doses of high-octane humour."

Pierre Trudeau diving on Tektite II.

MENTAL RESILIENCE
MASTERY OF FATIGUE, FRUSTRATION, AND FAILURE TO SUCCEED IN THE MISSION

"ARE YOU sure you want to dive with this breathing system?" asked the navy scientist.

"Sure, why not?" he said.

Pierre Elliott Trudeau extended his arms upward and a young man in khaki shorts lifted a large rectangular breathing unit onto his back and tightened its shoulder straps. The fifty-pound Mark 1 was the most advanced undersea breathing device ever built. Its white fibreglass shell contained electronic components similar to those used by Apollo astronauts. With each breath taken, a precise amount of oxygen was added and carbon dioxide removed. However, if one of its hundreds of components failed, a slow response by the diver could result in a loss of consciousness, and drowning.

We were sitting on the edge of a steel-hulled work barge in Greater Lamashur Bay in the US Virgin Islands. Beneath the water in front of us was the most ambitious undersea living experiment ever undertaken.

Tektite II was a five-million-dollar project funded by the United States government and a consortium of corporations and universities. Over a seven-month period, fifty-three scientists in five-person teams were spending up to four weeks at a time in the large, four-room station at a depth of 50 feet.

Tektite II had two objectives—a long-duration study of the ocean, and preparation for distant journeys in space. Most of its participants were marine scientists, but one was a NASA human factors engineer working on space station design. Everyone ate astronaut food and was under constant video scrutiny by NASA psychologists.

The Tektite scientists spent up to ten hours a day in the water. Geologists were studying the dynamics of sea-floor sediments; biologists were observing the practise of tropical fish communities and the vulnerability of coral reefs to pollution. They were pooling their fragments of hard-won information into an understanding of life on the nearby reefs and the great ocean beyond.

Trudeau looked the water below his swim fins. He had long, dark hair, sideburns, and blazing blue eyes. A few steps behind him, his muscular Royal Canadian Mounted Police bodyguard was frowning. In a few minutes, the Prime Minister of Canada would vanish into a world where he could not protect him.

Trudeau was one of those coolly competent individuals with an encyclopedic mind. The professor of law at the University of Montreal was elected to the House of Commons in his mid-forties. Soon after, he became minister of justice and won passage of two challenging policies—strict gun control legislation and reform of the laws regarding abortion and homosexuality. His colourful personality, self-effacing manner, and powerful speeches swept him into office on a wave of "Trudeaumania." In his first year, his cabinet created a new Ministry of Science and Department of the Environment.

Six months before, I had been invited to join him on a scuba diving vacation in Belize. He spent most of his time reading thick briefing books, but made hour-long dives in the morning and afternoon. One morning I saw him hold his breath, swim down forty feet, study the contours of a French angelfish, and swim back to the surface. A few minutes later, he repeated the process. We made eight scuba dives together; on our last descent we touched down briefly at 250 feet.

Politics was a hard game for a French-speaking anti-separatist from Quebec who wanted to establish diplomatic relations with China and create a new Canadian constitution. Trudeau coped with the stress—and his numerous setbacks—by having a sustained commitment to a firm set of values. He also designed his life around his daily workout and weekend exercises like canoeing and cross-country skiing. When his schedule allowed, he took short vacations to test his skills against a river, a mountain or the ocean. Knowing his interest in the ocean and the new technologies we were using to explore it, I invited him to visit Tektite II.

"Ready?" I asked.

"Let's go."

I slid into the water and turned toward him. Holding his fins flat to steady his entry, he dropped in beside me. Two safety divers wearing conventional scuba gear moved into position behind us. We exhaled and began our descent.

The first thing we saw was the undersea station positioned on the sand next to an escarpment of coral. Its two circular steel towers rose out of a large rectangular base giving it a stark, industrial look. A patina of green algae speckled its white paint.

Two members of the resident research team glided over the reef beneath us, heading toward the entrance hatch. They were twenty-four-hour residents of the ocean, their existence linked to the ebb and flow of undersea life. They'd seen sunsets through a rippling distance of water and experienced the velvet rumble of an undersea earthquake. For everyone living inside Tektite, the ocean had turned into something intimate and wondrously ungraspable.

Our first stop was the observation cupola, a circle of ten rectangular windows emitting faint shafts of light on top of the first tower. We peered inside, swam the short distance to the second tower, descended to one of its large, domed view ports, and looked into the station's main control room. It was nine feet high and twelve feet in diameter. Around its curved walls were racks of gas analyzers, pressure gauges, and television monitors. On the far side of the control room a young engineer sat at a desk writing in a notebook. Nearby was the tunnel leading to the other tower.

Tektite II was the Cadillac of undersea stations. The three adjoining rooms contained a laboratory, five bunks, a heat-and-serve galley, a stereo system, and a fresh-water shower. A central air conditioner maintained the atmosphere — 9 percent oxygen in 91 percent nitrogen — at a relatively dry 80 degrees Fahrenheit (26 degrees Celsius).

This was the tenth mission in the seven-month program. Moving his fins back and forth effortlessly, Trudeau peered through the hemispheric view port as if trying to understand the scientific and political meaning of the submerged station, its research projects, and the great ocean surrounding it.

THE NEXT day, as we flew back to Canada, Trudeau talked about the future of the global ocean. He was concerned about ocean pollution, especially in the Arctic. "When the Americans sent the USS *Manhattan* through our Northwest Passage," he told me, "it forced us to review our northern sovereignty and environmental policies."

At one point he tilted his head to one side and asked, "How about coming to Ottawa and help us put together a national ocean policy?" He knew I'd have a hard time fitting in with policy mavens and droning discussions in dimly lit rooms, so he waited to let the question sink in. "You'll learn a lot about the challenges of government," he said. At first I hesitated, but as an emerging student of leadership, I knew I had to accept his offer to serve my country

One month later I became a consultant to Michael Pitfield, a brilliant thinker who headed the Privy Council Office. My first task was to write a brief on all the ocean activities in Canada. I studied documents, interviewed senior civil servants, and wrote sections on industry, fishing, science, transportation, and naval operations. As the months passed, I began to understand how difficult it was to govern millions of people living in the world's second biggest country. I spent time in the Ministry of Science and the Department of the Environment. Those four years next to "the engine room" of government were an incomparable education in the complexities of political leadership.

During my first year I suggested to Pitfield that Canada's sovereignty position might be strengthened if we conducted a series of research expeditions (described in the first pages of this book) under the ice of the Northwest Passage. "It would be best to start with small teams and build from there," I told him. "We'll develop the systems and techniques to enable scientists to work safely under the polar ice pack. We'll integrate our human factors research with marine biology and geology." After many discussions and hard questions, the gears of government began to grind slowly.

Trudeau, Pitfield, and other senior officials became my mid-career role models and mentors. They explained the long, frustrating procedures that went with creating policies for so many people with so many competing interests. They supported me during the delays and failures of my Arctic research expeditions. They reminded me that true "exploration" is a strategically imagined benefit to society that comes by generating new knowledge and new relationships. It didn't matter if you were working in Ottawa or under the ice. You had to confront obstacles, uncertainties, and conflicting choices. You had to become a specialist in "makeshift" and keep moving forward.

REFLECTIONS ON MENTAL RESILIENCE

Mishaps are like knives that either serve us or cut us, as we grasp them by the blade or the handle.
—JAMES RUSSELL LOWELL

MENTAL RESILIENCE—the mastery of fatigue, frustration, and failure to succeed in the mission—is an essential leadership trait that complements all the others. Trudeau knew frustration and failure in his politics and his marriage. Honesty, humility, and magnanimity shaped his mental resilience.

No matter how hard you plan, how carefully you craft the use of your technology, how thoroughly you brief your team, something will go wrong. Adversity (any condition of adverse fortune) ranges in scale from savage weather to sullen technology to the sudden death of someone you're responsible for. When you're responsible for *everyone*, you need composure, perspective, and a handbrake on your heart rate.

When you come to the end of your rope, tie a knot and hang on.
—FRANKLIN D. ROOSEVELT

Leadership is not for the faint of heart. You mentally rehearse every aspect of the mission. Your mantra is: study, practise, and learn. You eat, sleep, and breathe teamwork. You struggle to act in the face of uncertainty. You live under the constant shadow of failure.

Good leaders need a grasp of economic realities, the political process, and the frameworks supporting science and technology. You don't need to know everything, just enough to measure what you're doing in the wider context, just enough to prepare for the unexpected.

I went to the Arctic on my first expedition with only three people on my team. I tried things out in a limited way and got lots of feedback from my teammates and government officials. I learned what happens when you live on an ice-rimmed shore, spend hours under ice-covered waters, and closely observe what you find there. This "safe-fail" method taught me that it's better to start small and make tiny, experimental mistakes. It also taught me that no matter what happens, learning itself is a meaningful outcome.

BARACK OBAMA was elected by supporters who spoke of "remaking this nation" and felt that everything was possible. As time passed, this blue-sky vision gave way to the daily grind of governance, jammed meeting schedules, thick briefing books, and thousands of immediate concerns and compromises. The oratory that proved so powerful on the campaign trail was not so effective in a polarized capital. It would take almost two years, but Obama and his team discovered that big-goal transformations require big-goal resilience.

In ways we can't imagine, President Obama has repeatedly passed through the fire. On the CBS program *60 Minutes* he described the tension he felt after giving the orders to send Seal Team 6 on their mission to kill Osama bin Laden: "These guys are going in the darkness of night. And they don't know what they're going to find there. They don't know if the building is rigged. They don't know if there are explosives that are triggered by a particular door opening. My number one concern was if I send them in can I get them out? . . . At the end of the day, this was still a 55/45 situation. We could not definitively say that bin Laden was there. Had he not been there, there would have been some significant consequences . . . You think about Black Hawk Down. You think about what happened with the Iranian rescue . . . you're making your best call, your best shot . . . I concluded that it was worth it . . . we have devoted enormous blood and treasure in fighting back against al Qaeda . . . And I said to myself if we had a good chance of badly disabling al Qaeda, then it was worth the political risks as well as the risks to our men."

The author's Rolex Submariner inside space shuttle *Endeavour*.

STRATEGIC IMAGINATION
MASTERY OF VISUALIZING PERFORMANCE IN THE NEAR AND FAR FUTURE

WE WERE standing alone on the deck of NASA's "beach house," a small, wood-panelled structure within sight of the Gulf Stream. To the north was the hazy outline of the space shuttle *Endeavour*, poised for tomorrow's journey to the International Space Station. The place was vibrant with history; every astronaut had come here before their mission to say goodbye to family and friends.

Shuttle astronaut Dr. Dave Williams is just over six feet tall. The powder blue T-shirt he wore that day covered the muscles of an NFL linebacker. As his six crewmates ate lunch inside, we talked about the three spacewalks he would undertake during his upcoming thirteen-day mission. I asked about the watch he was wearing. "NASA issue," he said, "What about yours?" I told him my Rolex Sea Dweller had been to some interesting places including the North Pole and the wreck of the *Titanic*.

He grinned. "Shall we give it a ride?"

"You're kidding."

His grin widened.

I couldn't get it off my wrist fast enough. He slipped it into his pocket and suddenly turned serious. "I'll take good care of it."

I MET Dave Williams while he was living in Aquarius, an undersea station off the coast of Florida. Operated by the US government, the ten-million-dollar facility had four bunks, a heat-and-serve galley, a computer section, and a wet lab. Most of the time marine scientists used it to study the health of nearby coral reefs, but on this mission Williams and two other astronauts were spending ten days inside, making long forays into the ocean to develop procedures for future space missions.

Williams was a Canadian physician at the peak of his profession when he embarked on a second career as an astronaut. His first mission was on *Columbia* in 1998. During his sixteen days in orbit, he and his crewmates studied the effects of microgravity on the brain and nervous system. After the flight he was appointed Director of Life Sciences at NASA, the first non-American to hold the position.

Since our handshake under the ocean Williams and I had become good friends. I visited him at the Johnson Space Center in Houston and talked to his crewmates. I watched him don an underwater version of a spacesuit and spend hours training in a pool containing sectional mock-ups of the shuttle and International Space Station.

I WAS two miles away when *Endeavour* began its gravity-defying journey. It exploded off the pad in a blast of sun-bright flame and rolling thunder. Eight minutes later, trailing a long column of bleached sky it approached its orbital velocity of 17,532 mph.

During his thirteen-day mission Williams made three six-hour spacewalks to assist in the construction of the space station. Prior to his first walk, he spent a night decompressing. The next morning he shrugged into his spacesuit, slipped out of the airlock, and climbed hand-over-hand to the outer end of the station. Working with his partner Rick Mastracchio, he guided a new section of structural spine—a five-thousand-pound aluminum truss—into position. Then, inches away from two major no-touch hazards, he secured its lockdown bolts.

On his second spacewalk, Williams balanced on the tip of the Canadarm, picked up a faulty 1200-pound gyroscope, swung out over the abyss and swapped it out with a new one from *Endeavour's* cargo bay. Looking down, he could see half a continent sliding sideways. Looking up, he could see all the way to Mars.

Inside the controlled cocoon of his spacesuit Williams heard nothing but the sound of his own breathing and the words spoken quietly into his headset by his crewmates. Every move he made was a focused convergence of muscular power and mental attention. The blinding sun and the black, bottomless sky transformed the station into something grand and fantastic. From its central spine to its solar panels, the difference between sunlight and shadow was as clean and sharp as the sun itself. Earth, so vast and blue, was very far away.

"As the sun dropped below the horizon," he told me after the mission, "I paused to savour the moment. Below was a spectacular view of the Pacific. Above it was a different kind of blue—the thin layer of the earth's atmosphere. Everywhere else was blackness, total blackness. The only lights were in the shuttle's payload bay. I was in total darkness on the end of the arm. As Charlie Hobaugh continued to swing me through space on the robotic arm I told him, "This is incredible! It's the smoothest ride of my life!" Charlie chuckled quietly, "Dave, it's on auto."

DURING THE years that preceded those thirteen days, Williams and his crewmates built an invisible web of competence and collaboration. They pictured their performance in the near and far future: strategic imagination was central to their efforts. The clear vision of what they wanted to achieve energized every challenge.

Long hours of labour were given gladly. The force of their imagination pushed them through every minor and major problem.

It started when they were young. They imagined being proficient at something and built the discipline and determination to bring it into being. At the age of seven, Williams imagined being an explorer. When he was thirteen he became a certified scuba diver and began exploring the ocean. A few years later he imagined being a physician. He struggled through medical school and became an expert in emergency care medicine. A successful medical doctor in his forties, he strategically imagined being an astronaut.

Each of Williams's three spacewalks tested his body's physical and mental limits. Moving his arms and legs inside his semi-rigid suit for six hours required the physical effort of an Olympic athlete. Ensuring his hands, feet, and fingertips were perfectly coordinated required the choreographed precision of a prima ballerina. And monitoring his life-support systems, his specific task, and updates from his crewmates required the mental concentration of an orchestra conductor.

From his precarious place in the heavens, Williams glanced down and saw the full curve of the earth. Every forty-five minutes he passed through a sunrise or a sunset. A deep-thinking man, he understood that he existed in this lethal place by virtue of three things: the thousands of people on the earth below him who built the machines that sustained him; the nine other men and women in orbit with him, and the strategic imagination that had driven his dream of becoming an undersea and space explorer.

Those seventeen hours inside his spacesuit were among the most intense and satisfying he would ever experience. He had imagined them and trained for them. They were the highlight of his contribution to the international team moving the human family beyond its planet of origin. Within them lay the meaning of his existence.

Three weeks after his mission Williams came to Toronto with his crewmates, and I interviewed him for a CBC radio program called *Ideas*. Before I turned on my digital recorder, he handed me my Rolex. "It's flown five million miles at seven times the speed of sound. Thanks for being such a great mentor."

For me, the beauty of his last sentence was that the roles of mentor and student had been reversed. Our hundreds of research dives under the Arctic Ocean including the construction of the first manned polar station and the discovery of the northernmost-known shipwreck had inspired Williams to imagine himself as an explorer and begin a long, arduous journey. Years later, in an undersea station off the coast of Florida, in the NASA training pool in Houston and in the hours before his second mission, he gave me intimate views of what it takes to step through an airlock and perform high-risk tasks at 17,532 miles an hour. The watch on my wrist confirms that deep leadership is mentorship flowing in reciprocal directions.

REFLECTIONS ON STRATEGIC IMAGINATION

Imagination, not invention, is the supreme master of art as of life.
— JOSEPH CONRAD

STRATEGIC IMAGINATION — the mastery of visualizing performance in the near and far future — is a conversation between your brain and your body. You concentrate your mind and use your visual, auditory, and kinaesthetic senses to rehearse a future activity and its options. It's a vital component of precision planning. To make it effective, you practise it regularly.

The strategic imagination required to carry out complex and dangerous missions is hard work. It's not a passive act; it's a sustained process of consciously organizing remembered events and observations into new conceptual frameworks. It requires understanding relationships, grasping differences and similarities, and abstracting parts of the whole into new concepts. It means drawing inferences, making deductions, reaching conclusions, asking difficult questions, and discovering new and sometimes strange answers. The faculty that directs this process is deep thinking. There is a risk. It comes from knowing that in spite of the heat generated by the neurons in your cerebral cortex, you might be terminally wrong.

On February 1, 2003, *Columbia* was torn apart on re-entry, killing all seven astronauts. The board of inquiry said that the direct cause was damage from a foam tile that came off during liftoff. A more basic cause was the NASA culture. As in the 1986 *Challenger* disaster, diligence about safety had been slowly replaced by low-profile complacency. Potential safety problems tended to be labelled as "insignificant" so that they wouldn't require fixes and cause delays. This flawed practice became embedded in the system, continued for years, and contributed to both accidents. According to one safety expert, *Challenger* and *Columbia* were lost because of a lack of strategic imagination.

Scott Carpenter described safety this way. "Safety for the astronaut was a paramount rule in Project Mercury. We astronauts were willing to take a few extra chances in order to get moving; that's the way we were built. But our bosses had their eyes on a bigger picture. They were not willing to let us take a chance on anything they felt might jeopardize the mission. All of life is, of course, a compromise. And what we were doing was life at the fullest."

Bold decisions and acts of genius arise from long and hard reflection. How will you perform?

How will your team partners perform? What can you do to improve their performance? When you arm yourself with this kind of forethought you create the confidence necessary for decisive action. You move forward unhindered by hesitation and half-heartedness.

You can mentally prepare for every demanding event by strategically imagining the place where you will perform, the people you will be with, the physical and mental energy you require, the objectives you want to achieve, and the activity needed to accomplish your objectives. You see yourself in your mind's eye, consciously guiding yourself toward a future action with a specific end.

To the blind, everything is sudden.
—ANONYMOUS

Williams and his crewmates are the current embodiment of "the right stuff." Their strategic imagination includes constant situational and peripheral awareness. They remind us that it won't just be rocket engines that put historic bootprints in the red dust of Mars. It will be new forms of leadership and teamwork—tomorrow's version of the right stuff.

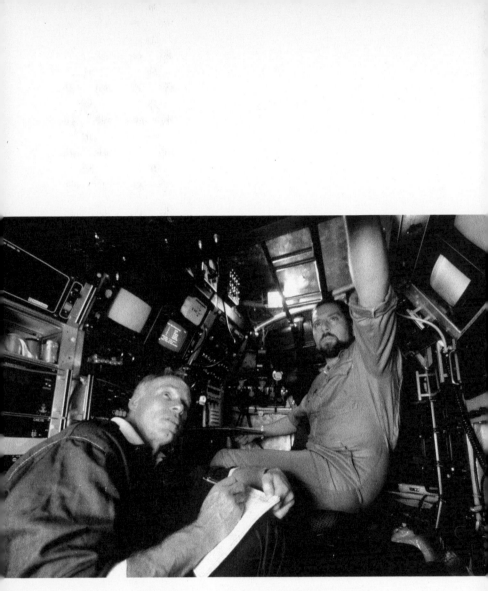

The author inside the research sub *Nautile*.

HIGH-EMPATHY COMMUNICATION
MASTERY OF RESPONDING TO THE UNSPOKEN NEEDS OF YOUR TEAMMATES

"TOMORROW YOU'LL dive to *Titanic* with two of the best men on my team. Jean-Michel will be your pilot and Pierre-Yves your copilot. It will be a long dive—three hours to the sea floor, six hours on the wreck, and three hours back to the surface."

I was standing on the deck of the French government research vessel *Nadir* looking into the blue eyes of Paul-Henri Nargeolet, a former French naval commander. In the shadows over his shoulder, his team of sub pilots, engineers, and technicians was preparing *Nautile*, their twenty-million-dollar research sub, for the next day's dive.

Nargeolet was tall and muscular with a movie-star smile. He knew every inch of his ship and his sleek yellow sub. Fluent in French, English, and Spanish, he communicated as easily with gestures as he did with words.

Nargeolet was tough, proud, and focused. He respected sailors and sub pilots, men like himself who were willing to put it all on the line to get the job done. He'd seen the immutable forces of the ocean—the wind, the waves, the currents, and the pressures—shape the character of those who worked in its depths. He had an old and visceral conviction that exploration was the business of daring individuals.

His military background served him well. He possessed competence and character. He made quick decisions and valued the contributions of others. He shared his team's worries and hardships. For Nargeolet, being a leader was not a role; it was who he was. The men in his team revered him and emulated his attitudes and behaviour.

Because a deep-sea research ship is jammed with sailors, scientists, and technicians, it's a place of contained but powerful emotions. And when a ten-ton submarine is lowered into a moving ocean, the tension soars. Nargeolet continuously assessed the mood swings of his team and tried to channel them in a positive way.

As we walked toward the sub, Nargeolet put his hand on my shoulder. "It's your first dive to *Titanic*, but don't worry. My team will take care of you in ways that will surprise you."

THE NEXT morning I climbed down through *Nautile's* narrow hatch. Its combat-tight crew sphere was filled with dozens of dials, gauges, and switches. There was a central control stick and three forward-looking view ports. I positioned myself on the thin cushion on the starboard side and my knees almost touched my chest.

Then Jean-Michel and Pierre-Yves slid in beside me. As they began going through their checklist, I realized I was descending two and a half miles under the ocean's surface to explore the Mount Everest of shipwrecks with two men I hardly knew.

The hatch closed and we were lowered over the stern of the ship into the cold North Atlantic. Minutes later, Jean-Michel emptied the ballast chambers and *Nautile* began a long, gravity-driven free fall.

It took almost three hours to get to the *Titanic*. We dropped through the Gulf Stream and the Labrador Current, and the ocean got colder and blacker. The air was heavy with processed oxygen, scrubbed carbon dioxide, and working sweat. I glanced out the porthole into a universe of darkness filled with the glowing bioluminescence of microscopic creatures. As the crew cabin groaned with the increasing pressures, the hair stood up on the back of my neck. When it comes to this kind of depth, I have a PhD in fear.

As we passed six thousand feet I took a long look at the electrical panels and junction boxes in the crew cabin. They contained hundreds of feet of wiring and hundreds of electrical connections. If a single connection overheated, the fire and smoke would immediately fill our lungs.

Jean-Michel looked at the sweat gleaming on my forehead, glanced at his watch and grinned. It was the infectious smile of a French pilot who knew he had an alpha coward in his sub.

As we dropped through nine thousand feet I thought about the giant rust-hulk of the ship below us. It was surrounded by torn pieces of metal and thick tangles of wire. The ocean would be tomb-black, filled with unpredictable currents. We might get swept into a snarl of heavy-gauge wire. Twenty years later wide-eyed observers in tourist subs would be whispering: "Those are the guys who never made it."

When we reached the sea floor, Jean-Michel flew over the tan-coloured sediments and gently parked the sub. Then he leaned forward, opened an aluminum drawer, brought out three plastic containers, and placed them on our laps. Inside were open-faced sandwiches and a small bottle of Beaujolais Blanc. Jean-Michel looked at his watch, smiled, and said, "Monsieur Joe, we see zat you are a beet nervous, so we zink it is time for zee peekneek."

We sat on the bottom of the Atlantic Ocean eating the sandwiches and sipping the wine. We talked about French politics and French literature and I completely forgot where I was. Then, about twenty minutes later, it hit me. This was not just a picnic at the bottom of the Atlantic; this was a gift from Nargeolet. He knew I'd be anxious on my first dive, and that a Beaujolais Blanc lunch would give me confidence in the pilots and their hard-won skills.

This was communication beyond meetings and memos; this was anticipating and responding to the unspoken needs of someone you were responsible for.

We spent nine hours exploring the *Titanic*. I saw the giant boilers that powered the fifty-thousand-ton ship. I saw the debris field and hundreds of nautical and personal object that had spilled out of the interior when the ship broke apart. I saw the shattered stern where so many lives were lost. I was anxious, but my heart beat at a reasonable rate. I was with two men whose emotional awareness diminished my fear.

REFLECTIONS ON
HIGH-EMPATHY COMMUNICATION

DEEP LEADERS like Paul-Henri Nargeolet carefully track the changing contours of their followers' emotional intelligence. Their ability to observe objectively and listen closely gives them an intuitive grasp of the team's anxieties, moods, and needs.

BEYOND MOST meetings, memos, and tweets, there are moments of authentic communication. They are supported by invisible bridges of trust and confidence. We freely offer a part of ourselves, hoping it will be accepted. They are moments of potential and peril.

The best leaders have a soul-whispering empathy. They know their team partners so well that they read their minds, finish their sentences, and articulate their unspoken worries. This empathy is a foundation upon which they build their teams. As a result, their teams are bound together by professional skills, a sense of mission, and close friendships supported by random and excessive acts of kindness. The kindness runs like an electric current among them.

IN A COMMERCIAL office or military battlefield, leaders are never as much in charge as they are pictured to be, nor are followers ever as submissive as they seem. Insights, influence, and empathy flow both ways. This flow of ideas means that leadership is a conversation between minds. It also means that to a great extent, followers "make" the leader.

Astronauts develop a utilitarian empathy. During their training they develop the competence to imagine themselves in a crewmate's position and intuit his or her requirements. During their missions they climb into each other's minds and tune in to unspoken needs.

Each morning when he first saw me, the captain of the French research ship looked directly into my eyes, smiled, clasped my hands, and said, "*Bonjour, mon ami.*" He performed this ritual with everyone on the ship, from the youngest deckhand to his first mate. On the last day I asked him why he did this. "We're hundreds of miles from shore," he said. "It's my way of confirming that while we're out here I depend on you and you depend on me."

On the French ship, everyone was fully immersed in purposeful tasks, balanced between adrenalin and exhaustion. In spite of this, the mood on the ship was relaxed. If there was one thing everyone shared it was professional calm—a serenity born of confidence. No one knew their sub better than they did—on every dive they bet their lives on it.

During my time with the troops in Afghanistan, I learned the importance of "empathy when there are no answers." It came in the words of Carol Bateman, padre of the RCR Battle Group. She told me, "The worst moments are the ramp ceremonies and dealing with the friends of our fallen soldiers in the days after, in the days when they have to go back and walk that same road where their friend was blown up. When they struggle to ask why did this happen to him or to her? Why didn't we see it? And there are no answers. Those are the really tough moments, when there are no answers."

Anatoly Sagalevitch and Jim Cameron.

BLOOD TRUST
MASTERY OF THE HONESTY, INTEGRITY, AND LOYALTY THAT SUSTAINS THE TEAM

IT WAS a freezing February night. I was in Suzdhal, a medieval town north of Moscow, in a large, smoke-filled room crowded with Russian and American scientists. For three days we'd been discussing new undersea technologies and how they might advance deep-sea exploration. It was the final night of the conference; vodka was poured, toasts were made, and we were beyond exuberant. The only dour faces were the dark-suited men positioned around the perimeter of the room, watching us. The KGB operatives had wide shoulders short haircuts, and drill-bit eyes. They disliked the fact that Cold War enemies were discussing science and technology.

On everyone's mind was the recent loss of the Russian nuclear attack submarine *Komsomolets*. The runaway fire and freezing ocean had snuffed out the lives of half her crew. She was now lying on the sea floor under a mile of water. The Russian navy had surveyed the wreck and was piecing together the causes of the accident; Norwegian environmentalists were concerned that her reactor and nuclear torpedoes were a threat to the ocean.

At the end of the evening, a short, powerfully built man eased over to me and locked his eyes into mine. Anatoly Sagalevich led the Russian Academy of Sciences sub team and was the chief pilot of the *Mirs*, two twenty-million-dollar machines that could carry three people to a depth of twenty thousand feet. Six months earlier, he had invited me to join him on his research ship, the *Akademik Keldysh*, and sail across the Atlantic to Washington. North of the Azores, I slid inside *Mir 1* and we made a three-mile dive into a submerged canyon.

"We've been down to inspect *Komsomolets*," he said quietly. "My colleagues and I think its radioactivity might affect the North Sea fishery, but our navy is keeping everything quiet. We need your help. I have a videotape showing the sub on the sea floor. I'd like you to take it and tell the story in the West."

I glanced over his shoulder at the men in dark suits. If they found me with images of the nuclear sub they'd toss me into a van and ship me off to the nearest gulag. But Sagalevich's eyes had *that look*. Here was a man willing to put everything on the line — his career, his family, his life — for something he believed in. My mind raced back to a dive we'd undertaken in the eastern Atlantic north of the Azores, two years earlier.

We were inside a narrow, steep-walled canyon trying to recover geological samples. The canyon was 15,000 feet deep — three times as deep as the Grand Canyon and five times as deep as the two submersibles' previous dives had ever taken them.

Like *Nautile*, the *Mir* subs were marvels of engineering complexity. They had three propeller-driven thrusters, two mechanical arms, and a large, bottom-mounted battery. Sagalevich was the pilot and my crewmate was Emory Kristof, an acclaimed *National Geographic* photographer.

We were almost on the bottom, descending through the near-freezing water at a hundred feet a minute, when a sudden current swept the sub sideways and we slammed into the canyon wall. There was the crash of steel on stone, the sub tipped over and the lights went out, followed by the faint smell of something burning. For the first time in my life I discovered my heart could stop and I could still function.

My biggest fear was that the impact had torn away a thru-hull fitting and the full weight of the North Atlantic Ocean would burst into the crew cabin and turn the three of us into pink slurry.

In the darkness, Sagalevich checked the electrical system. I fought off my panic and confirmed the integrity of our oxygen supply. Kristof—breathing like a racehorse—checked the communication system. He and I had made dozens of dangerous dives together, including three beneath the ice at the North Pole. I knew that if things went wrong he'd save my life. And he, bless him, believed that I would save his.

At one point Kristof leaned into my ear and whispered a shot of hot-zone humour: "Don't worry, amigo, if that thru-hull fitting has sheared off and water comes screaming in here—the only thing you're gonna feel is my footprint on your forehead *trying to get out of here.*"

It was the best thing he could have said. My anxiety level was climbing into the stratosphere and I was on the edge of a Category 5 panic. The master of hot-zone humour was telling me that he was as anxious as I was and that we had to focus on the checklist that would get us back to the surface.

Minutes later—the longest year and a half of my life—we switched the lights back on and Sagalevich righted the sub and backed us away from the cliff. The second sub came in, inspected our pressure hull and said we looked okay. After a brief discussion and further system checks, we decided to finish the dive.

We survived because Sagalevich and Kristof were cool and competent. We survived because we needed and trusted each other.

THE MAN who had saved my life handed me the videotape. I slipped it into my pocket and slowly walked out of the room. Three days later I flew back to Toronto, spent four hours in an editing suite at the CTV network, and put together a short news release. The story was picked up by CNN, ABC, and NBC, and flashed around the world. We didn't know it at the time, but Sagalevich's story opened a small window into a major problem. During the Cold War, NATO and the Soviet Union had used the ocean as a nuclear dumping ground. Thousands of drums of nuclear waste were dropped into undersea canyons in places like Novaya Zemblya, Kamchatka, and the Farallon Islands off the coast of California. In addition, there were five nuclear submarines—two American and three Russian—lying on the floor of the ocean. Inside and outside those rusting subs were fifty nuclear warheads. Thanks to Sagalevich, Greenpeace, the Bellona Foundation, and many others, the dumping of nuclear waste is no longer permitted.

Sagalevich has many deep leadership traits including strategic imagination and mental resilience. Like all leaders, he has flaws. He can be arrogant and abrupt. He rarely laughs unless lit up by vodka. Brought up in the Soviet system, he's short on humility, gratitude, and fiscal responsibility. But when you're on his ship or inside his sub, you can count on his cool competence, blood trust, and physical robustness.

He was the right leader in the right place at the right time. He had a grasp of world and national affairs. He knew that Russia had to change. He extended a hand toward America when officials in the Kremlin thought the idea was treasonous. He learned English and made friends in Washington. Fighting a chronic lack of funds and harsh criticism from his colleagues, he built a world-class marine science sub team that could operate in any ocean in any weather. His energy, experience, and leadership, and the mutual trust he established with his American friends, were among the thousands of reasons the Berlin Wall came down.

REFLECTIONS ON BLOOD TRUST

You have to recognize tyranny and be willing to stand up against it. You have to be willing to fight for your beliefs. If you do that I'm going to see you at the barricades."
—BOBBY KENNEDY JR.

IN UNDERSEA exploration, we trust each other with our lives. If you tell me the sub is ready to dive, I believe you. When I tell you the carbon dioxide level is within safe limits, you believe me. Trust in each other is the backbone of our profession. It doesn't mean we won't make mistakes. We will. What it does mean is that when a mistake is made you will level with me and I will level with you. Our word is our bond. If we are honest with each other, we can handle anything. As author and former US secretary of education William J. Bennett says, "Loyalty is like courage; it shows itself most clearly when we are operating under stress. Real loyalty does not wither under assault."

JAMMED INTO the combat confines of the *Mir* crew sphere, my safety depended on interlocking circles of technology and trust, including the mother ship above me, the launch and recovery system that put us in the ocean, the life-support system that allowed us to breathe, the men on the mother ship tracking our every move, the deckhands operating the launch crane, and the soft-spoken man beside me steering us into the depths.

> The loyalty of your men is a sacred trust you carry. It is something that can never be betrayed.
>
> — ERNEST SHACKLETON

Sagalevich invited me to Moscow to visit his research laboratory and meet his family. He became my window into the sweeping political changes taking place in the Soviet Union and Eastern Europe. Some of his relatives were among the millions killed by the Second World War and Stalin's purges. He played songs on his guitar about friendship and tolerance. He was a fluent communicator with a hunger for facts. Watching him lead his team was like watching what Russia might become.

Deep leaders help their team partners navigate turbulent seas of change. They press for new skills, new behaviours, and new directions. They understand that people pushed out of their comfort zones get annoyed and angry. They know that earning respect is more important than being liked.

The best leaders find numerous ways of saying "I hear you; I understand you. I'm going to fight for you and do everything I can to make your job easier. You can trust me."

Sagalevich invited me to Siberia to write an article about the scientific research being done under the surface of Lake Baikal. Sailing along the mountain-rimmed coastline of the world's deepest lake, I discovered the poetry and prose of Yevgeny Yevtushenko. In Russia, poets are the voice of the people, champions of truth and justice, and catalysts for social change. Yevtushenko opened my eyes to the poet as leader. He wrote: "Let us not look for enemies among ourselves since we have common enemies—the threat of nuclear war, terrible natural catastrophes, ethnic conflicts, the economic crises, ecological disasters, and bureaucratic swamps."

Leadership is not just the responsibility of the people in the highest position. Everyone must participate in a dynamic relationship based on proficiency, personality, and trust.

Jim Cameron and his team
rehearse a dive.

FIERCE INGENUITY
MASTERY OF LATERAL THINKING TO SOLVE SEEMINGLY IMPOSSIBLE PROBLEMS

"THE ONLY way to solve the problem is to burn a hole in the side of your ship."

Captain Dennis sucked in his breath. "How big?" he asked.

"The size of a school bus."

The captain exhaled softly, gazed down at the deck, and then into the scowling face of the man in front of him.

The face belonged to Hollywood film director and deepsea explorer James Cameron. On this expedition, Cameron was directing a fourteen-million-dollar Disney IMAX film called *Aliens of the Deep*. At the heart of his story were young scientists using research subs to explore deep-sea volcanic vent systems, discovering the bizarre communities of life inside them, and speculating on the possibility of life in other parts of the solar system.

Cameron had invited me on board to write the companion book to the film. "Tell your story any way you want," he told me. "You'll have access to two large ships, four research subs, and a million-dollar videocam robot. You'll talk to a team of seventy scientists, engineers, and technicians from five universities, NASA, and the Russian Academy of Sciences."

Cameron is a great leader. He's got a high-bandwidth intelligence, thinks like a rebel, and knows exactly what he wants to achieve. He knows that the physical forces of the ocean can kill a project as easily as they can take a human life. Among his strongest leadership traits are precision planning and fierce ingenuity. His preparations are so thorough that he makes plans for his plans. On a deep-sea project there are hundreds of ways for things to go wrong and when that happens he wants to be ready to fast-map the options and apply fierce ingenuity.

Most of the dives we made during the two-month expedition were on the submerged ten-thousand-mile mountain range that runs down the centre of the Atlantic Ocean from the Arctic to the Antarctic. The mountains, with their steep hills and stark valleys, are among the most mysterious places on earth. It had taken two years, twenty-five million dollars and thousands of hours of searching with the most advanced undersea technology before French investigators working with Woods Hole Oceanographic found the remains of Air France Flight 447.

Two hundred and fifty million years ago the supercontinent Pangaea split into the seven continents we see today. The slowly stretching land mass tore fissures in the earth's crust, creating gaping canyons that spread apart to become today's oceans. Submerged volcanoes continued to erupt, pushing up magma and forming basaltic mountains as tall as the Andes but two miles deep. The mountains under the Atlantic were part of a fifty-thousand-mile, earth-girdling chain winding across the Southern Pacific and lower Indian Ocean.

Our major technical objective was to have all four subs rendezvous on the summit of one of the mountains and explore the strange life forms living there. It would be a technical first, provide spectacular scenes for the film, and for the NASA scientists on board, simulate a mission to Mars.

I had the good fortune to make a reconnaissance dive into the waters above the mountain. It was as high as Mount Rainier and its summit had a small plateau three thousand feet below the surface.

On the day of the big dive, I was standing on the deck next to Cameron as we launched the transparent-hulled *Deep Rover* submersibles. As we picked up the first six-ton sub and were slowly lowering it over the stern, there was the smell of burning hydraulic fluid. The crane made a strange groaning sound, and shuddered to a stop. We ran over to see what had happened. It was an "Oh, shark!" moment. The main hydraulic piston was jammed and beyond repair.

We were in the middle of the ocean with two subs on deck and no way to get them into the water.

Standing next to the launch crane in his sweat-stained T-shirt, Cameron was so angry he looked like a funnel cloud searching for a trailer park. But his anger was short-lived. He had a multimillion-dollar project resting on his shoulders and had to come up with a solution. Right now. On the spot. He took a long look at the other machinery on the deck and huddled with his launch crew.

Like all deep leaders, Cameron understands that his most critical and constrained resource is time. How he chooses to spend it determines his effectiveness. He knows when to delegate and when he must personally focus on a high-payoff challenge. He also knows that distractions and interruptions are the enemy of innovation. There are moments when you have to go into a room alone, close the door behind you, and wrestle with a problem.

Cameron went up to the survey room on the second deck, sat down with a pencil and yellow notepad, and attacked the engineering challenge with his trademark intensity. The subs would be launched over the side of the ship instead of the stern. Three men would modify a mid-deck cargo crane. Three others would re-rig the capstans and winches and network of lines to keep the subs from swinging when the ship rolled. Two experts with cutting torches would burn a rectangular hole—the size of a school bus—in the half-inch steel plate on the starboard side of the ship.

Everyone from Captain Dennis to the ship's engineer knew that you never cut a hole in the side of your ship, even when it's above the waterline, but they also knew this was a time to break the rules. The weather was good and the steel plate would be returned to its rightful place. Two days later we had a makeshift launch system. We tested it by lifting a heavy cage and trying to lower it into the sea. The ship rolled and the cage slammed into the ship's superstructure. We made adjustments. On one test a handling line snapped and the *Deep Rover* crashed onto the deck. Finally, after six trial runs, with bruised shins and patches of scraped skin oozing red, we were ready.

On the day of the four-sub dive the two *Mirs* descended from their mother ship and located a small plateau near the summit of the mountain. An hour later, the *Rovers* navigated through a field of white limestone towers and parked beside them. For the next two hours, ten scientists, sub pilots, and filmmakers used a suite of cameras to capture the wonder of the ancient, animated ocean.

Cameron was in the lead *Deep Rover*, directing all four subs and the videocam robot that flew off the bow of *Mir 1* to do some downslope exploring. Later, as I watched the footage taken inside and outside the subs, it was clear that even at three thousand feet down, Cameron's "charisma" carried the day.

Some leaders have it; others don't. The best leaders have it in abundance. Deep down, every leader wants it. This inner strength, this "gift of grace," an enthusiastic, positive approach to life, strikes a chord in others and brings out the best in them.

Charisma is the basis of "transformational" leadership. It's a synthesis of behaviours that enables certain leaders to become inspiring role models for their followers. They are admired and respected because of their extraordinary capabilities and determination. They are consistent, take risks, and have high standards.

At the core of charisma is a deep concern for others, an understanding of what makes people tick—as a team and as individuals. Despite appearances, Cameron had it in spades. He was intensely loyal to anyone who had given his or her best to one of his projects. He had a remarkable ability to select the right actors for his movies and the right participants for his expeditions; he could bring out their finest performances. Early in his career, if you had been the object of one of his withering tirades, you would have been sure he didn't give a damn about people's feelings. But as time went on he turned his introspective eye on himself, and his temper became a thing of the past.

The dive, the expedition, and the film succeeded because one man planned with precision and then, blindsided by a technical breakdown, fast-mapped the problem, listed the options, selected the best one, and applied fierce ingenuity and furious effort. And inspired the rest of us to follow him.

REFLECTIONS ON FIERCE INGENUITY

GREAT LEADERS are locked in, focused, and self-contained. In an age of instant messaging, multitasking, wireless distractions, and attention deficit disorder, they are exemplars of mental discipline. They know how to enter a cocoon of concentration and use lateral thinking to solve deadline-driven problems.

In the months prior to the expedition, Cameron tried to prepare for every contingency. He wrote a long list of standard operational procedures. He wrote an equally long list of emergency operational procedures. He selected a versatile, collaborative team. He knew that if he ended up in a lifeboat without food or water he wanted men with the genius to create both.

Deep leaders are all-terrain watchers, especially when it comes to people. They see who's got the juice and who hasn't. They notice who's working, who's slacking, and who's got iron discipline and determination. They're attracted to other lateral thinkers.

Distractions are the enemy of ingenuity and innovation. Fight back. Find a quiet place. Free your mind from interruptions.

Cameron doesn't just describe solutions to problems. He brings out a pencil and paper and draws them. It brings clarity and truth to his thinking. He also knows people want to see exactly what the new arrangement looks like.

From the beginning, his *Aliens of the Deep* expedition was plagued by electrical-mechanical problems. Fitting the new 3D-HD cameras into the *Deep Rover* subs took five times as long as it was supposed to. Relay switches and circuit boards on the *Deep Rovers* kept failing. In spite of this, Cameron's attitude was positive; visible misery was never an option.

When you go to sea you want to know who's running the ship. If the wind blows at fifty knots and the waves are as high as two-storey houses, your life is in his or her hands. The best captains are the confident, competent ones who admit to failure and understand the need for fierce ingenuity.

To prepare for the hard moments, you master all the details. There are hundreds, maybe thousands of them and they contain the truth about your state of readiness. Ignore them and you expose yourself to hasty and superficial decisions.

Deep leaders like Jim Cameron appear to be larger-than-life figures. In fact, they are the sum total of their individual perceptions, judgments, experiences, and insights. They are reminders that no matter how young or old you are, your job is to think hard—learn everything you can learn and understand everything you can understand. They are reminders that life is all about perfection of performance, about striving to figure out what you are doing and how you can do it better.

AUTHOR AND psychiatrist Edward M. Hallowell stresses that "fear disables the mind just as surely as lack of oxygen." Everyone has had low-oxygen moments that were resolved by the lateral thinking of fierce ingenuity. The beauty of bad times is that they focus our minds, forcing us to find new options and new opportunities. Don't just think beyond the box. Think beyond the building. Flirt with the impossible.

Jacques Cousteau.

TEAM GENIUS
MASTERY OF SOLVING MISSION-CRITICAL PROBLEMS WITH FAST, ELEGANT, SHARED SOLUTIONS

"THIS MORNING one of our *Calypso* divers died in the St. Lawrence River. I'm hoping you might help us find out what happened."

Jacques-Yves Cousteau was on the phone from Paris. He told me that three men were filming a shipwreck in low visibility water when one of them suddenly disappeared. He was found an hour later lying face down on the riverbed. The anguish in Cousteau's voice was palpable.

The acclaimed undersea pioneer, who opened the sunlit depths of the ocean to millions of divers, was one of my leadership exemplars. When I was in medical school he was my role model; his books and films inspired me to become an undersea physician. Years later he became a mentor; as medical director of Ocean Systems, I spent time with him in his Marseille research lab. His sons Philippe and Jean-Michel became good friends of mine.

I told him it would take me three hours to get to his ship.

During the drive, I thought about how the charismatic Frenchman had used films to alter our understanding of the ocean. As captain of the *Calypso*, he led teams that made the Academy Award–winning documentary *The Silent World* and three successful prime-time television series. That summer, he was producing a two-hour documentary about North America's

Great Lakes and the mighty river that carried them to the sea.

The ocean made Cousteau. His luck was to be in the right place at the right age with the right intelligence, commitment, and hard-won skills. He was a sea captain who could dive and write. He was a magnetic public speaker and filmmaker. In his Conshelf undersea station experiments, he considered the complexities and ambiguities of the ocean, consulted with engineers and scientists, made the right decisions, and led his teams with clear objectives.

Cousteau was a master of persuasion, a leader who leveraged his success with the sea into a performance of personality. On board *Calypso* he wore a blue denim shirt and a red watch cap; on land he donned exquisitely tailored suits and his trademark white silk turtleneck. Then there were the calculated mannerisms: the graceful walk across the deck to gaze at the horizon and the effortless entry into the sea at the beginning of every dive. Finally, there was his elegant French accent with its lyrical cadence and reflective pauses.

Cousteau brought to life numerous engineering ideas, but his greatest invention was himself. He understood the power of embedding his name in the public imagination and keeping it visible. He played the media with consummate skill, carefully arranging his words in short poetic sentences. The master of powerful presentations understood the potency of a dramatic photograph of a great white shark or an ancient Mediterranean shipwreck. At heart, Cousteau was a spellbinding storyteller.

SOME YEARS ago, I went on board *Calypso* in the old harbour in Nice, France. It was a warm summer day and her main deck was empty. I peered through the windows of a room stretching the width of the deck. The air was filled with the blue smoke of

Gauloise cigarettes. On both sides of a long table covered with food and bottles of wine, men were making jokes and talking about the day's work. There were young faces projecting strength and older faces weathered from days in the sun. These were men who swam into an alien world and found themselves at home.

At the centre of the table was Cousteau's slim, taut face with its enigmatic smile. Even in casual conversation, he was a grand synthesizer, blending art and science in arresting ways.

"The team is everything," he once told me. "Our routines on the ship and our dives under the ocean are designed for maximum collaboration. We join our ideas together, the good ones, the bad ones, each one informing the next, until we find a solution that works. It takes time. It's slow and inefficient." He shrugged. "But it works."

To see Cousteau and his team sitting around the table, drinking wine, listening closely to each other's words, was to witness a fluid dynamic of gestures and conversation. Each participant played off the other, every verbal contribution . . . "*Oui, oui . . .*" providing the spark for the next idea. The chorus of voices created something more original and complex than one man could fashion alone.

Cousteau once told me two important things he'd learned from long days at sea. "The ocean reminds us that everything we do in life is collaboration," he told me. "The ocean demands the right balance of planning, structure, and improvisation."

CALYPSO WAS moored alongside a pier in Kingston harbour. At the same table where the men had been drinking wine and telling jokes, Cousteau's son Jean-Michel described the accident. With his help I spent the next two days trying to find out where the balance of planning, structure, and improvisation had gone wrong. I interviewed the crew, spoke with police officers conducting an investigation, and went to the Kingston hospital to study the autopsy findings. Slowly, the events that took place inside the river's dark waters began to emerge.

Two divers were filming a nineteenth-century shipwreck at a depth of 120 feet. One was carrying a camera; the other was carrying a movie light powered by a generator in a small boat. A third diver was in the water at a depth of sixty feet moving the generator cable sideways for the diver with the light. New to the team, he was working hard to make a good impression. He'd not slept well the night before and had skipped breakfast; fatigue and low blood sugar may have slowed his judgment. Struggling to keep the tension in the cable, he inadvertently held his breath. Unknowingly, he made a short ascent. The air in his lungs expanded, slid into his blood stream, and sent bubbles into his brain. He lost consciousness and drifted downward until he came to rest on the riverbed.

I called Cousteau in Paris and told him what I'd found.

"Such a tragedy for his family," he said. "Such a tragedy for the team. We must find the lesson in this."

REFLECTIONS ON TEAM GENIUS

SO MUCH of what we do under the ocean and in other lethal environments hinges on choices made by instinct—in an instant—with consequences that last a lifetime. The task of the leader and the team is to do whatever it takes to be ready to make the right choice when those hot-zone moments arrive.

A special kind of creativity—team genius—occurs when people who have mastered two or more different fields use the framework of one to ignite fresh thoughts about the other.

Cousteau's breakthrough ideas about exploration, films, and engineering were embedded in years of false starts, improvisations, and tight interactions with talented people. He surrounded himself with experts in marine engineering, diving and marine biology. His long relationship with trial, error, and talent continually improved his ability to make wiser, more confident decisions.

Creativity comes to a team when it has a broad education and is comfortable with ideas, abstractions, and self-doubt. Its members switch back and forth from concepts to uncertainty to completion. They possess a relentless ability to learn.

In his human factors research lab in Marseille, Cousteau established a creative space where innovation could flourish. His team of physicians, technicians, and divers helped each other negotiate biological and engineering choke points, and generate synergy-driven solutions. Author and professor Keith Sawyer tells us that collective ownership of a task allows divisions between team members to break down and spurs everyone to perform at higher levels. Watching Cousteau's team toil inside and outside their huge recompression chamber, surrounded by cylinders of high-pressure oxygen, nitrogen, and helium, was like seeing musicians at work. They were not playing for an audience; they were playing for each other.

WE OFFER our lives to machines that carry us into space and into the ocean. They sometimes show us that things can go shockingly wrong. The culprit is never a single event; the culprit is almost always multiple failures and mistakes—a lethal combination of poor maintenance, shortcuts, and bad communication. Slowly, invisibly, the strain builds. The leader's responsibility is to monitor the strain, anticipate the breaking point, get the message to his team, and avoid the disaster.

> So when a good idea comes, part of my job is to move it around, just see what different people think, get people talking about it, argue with people about it, get ideas moving among that group of one hundred people, get different people together to explore different aspects of it quietly, and—just explore things.
>
> —STEVE JOBS

Team genius—the mastery of mission-critical problems with fast, elegant, shared solutions—is enhanced by many of the other deep leadership traits. Think of it as a blue-ribbon blend of cool competence, high-empathy communication, and blood trust. At the heart of my definition of team genius is the word *shared*. Concepts and tentative conclusions shift back and forth between partners until the right solution is discovered. It's reciprocal learning—not unlike the swift and subtle art of mentoring.

When you're four thousand metres below the ocean or in a forward operating base in Afghanistan, there are two fundamental rules that define the relationship between you and the person beside you. The first rule is: take care of each other. The second rule is: take care of each other.

Buzz Aldrin on the moon.

RESOLUTE COURAGE
MASTERY OF MAKING DIFFICULT, DANGEROUS, LONG-DURATION DECISIONS

"AS NEIL and I stood on the moon with Mike Collins in orbit, it was so inspiring to think that the three of us were further away than humans had ever been. But it was really eerie knowing what we had to do to get back."

I was standing on a snow-covered slope in the Rocky Mountains with Buzz Aldrin. He was of medium height and had the solid grace of a much younger man. Not quite the thirty-nine-year-old astronaut who left those famous bootprints on the moon, but you get the idea. He looked at me with eyes that had seen the earth suspended in the sky a quarter of a million miles away.

"The moon is a magnificent place for humans to go back to and make use of," he said, "but it's very desolate. That's why I used the words 'magnificent desolation,' when I stepped on its surface."

After graduating from the Military Academy at West Point, Aldrin joined the United States Air Force, flew sixty-six combat missions in Korea, and served in West Germany. He earned a PhD from MIT with a dissertation describing the orbital mechanics of spacecraft. Soon after, he became a NASA astronaut.

In 1966 he and Jim Lovell completed a four-day flight in the Gemini 12 space capsule, and made a five-hour spacewalk. In early 1969, Aldrin was selected for the first moon-landing team.

I was at Cape Canaveral to write a feature article for the *Toronto Telegram* when Apollo 11 began its long, uncertain journey. I felt the ground shake and watched the white rocket rise up on a column of orange flame and thunder into the heavens.

Years later, I met Aldrin on a scuba diving trip in the Bahamas. He never talked about the physical and mental courage it took to fly through space and set a small spacecraft down on the rocky surface of the moon. For him, courage was contained inside other concepts like discipline, initiative, and trust. Courage meant making hard, independent decisions when the situation suddenly changed. And when the moon's grey surface was two thousand feet below his spacecraft and closing fast, the situation suddenly changed.

Through the forward window, Aldrin and Armstrong saw their flight computer was going to put them down in a boulder field that would shear off the Lander's legs. Armstrong took over the controls and manually flew over one hazardous site and then another. Lights started blinking, abort alarms started ringing, and fuel levels went critical. As Aldrin read out the descent rate and fuel consumption, Armstrong's heart rate soared into triple digits. Finally, he saw a safe place and touched down. Both men were hyperventilating. They had twenty seconds of fuel remaining. After catching his breath, Armstrong told the world that "*Eagle* has landed at Tranquility Base."

The two men were the first humans to set foot on a celestial body other than Earth. Their feat, witnessed by the largest worldwide television audience in history, was one of humankind's greatest technical achievements. In the four decades since, millions of people have had their earth-centred perspectives altered by the iconic photograph of Aldrin standing on the moon in a white spacesuit.

The resolute courage that carried Aldrin to the moon and back was embedded in trust. Trust in his own character and competence and that of his crewmates. Trust in the advanced rocket technology and the people who built and maintained it. Trust in the systems thinking that allowed him and Armstrong to see things in terms of *what was really happening* rather than relying on *what should be happening.*

Apollo 11 made Aldrin one of the most famous people on the planet, but after his year-long public relations tour he was a man without direction or purpose. The demons of depression and alcoholism took over and he burned through two marriages, ingloriously ended his air force career, and began selling cars for a living. "Magnificent desolation" described the bleak terrain of his life.

After years of drifting, Aldrin confronted his depression and alcoholism and fought to become sober. He made peace with his family, and became a tireless advocate for the future of space exploration.

When I saw him in Banff, Alberta, we were participating with two hundred others in a fundraising event for Bobby Kennedy Jr.'s Waterkeeper Alliance. A few minutes earlier we had raised our glasses to celebrate Aldrin's birthday. By then his commitment to critical projects and his enjoyment of life confirmed how far it was possible to travel inside and outside oneself.

Aldrin was anxious to get back to the top of the mountain for another run. As we walked toward our skis, I asked him about NASA's next step in the human exploration of space. "We've got to lead where it matters most," he said, "and build the systems that safely transport humans across space. Most importantly, we should aim toward a permanent base on Mars within the next two decades."

Many months later I joined him at a small meeting in Washington where he gave an impassioned speech about his "Mars for America" project. "Forty years ago," he said, "Neil, Mike, and I began our quarter-million-mile journey through the blackness of space to reach the moon. Today, no nation, including our own, is capable of sending anyone beyond Earth's orbit. For the past four years NASA has been on a path to resume lunar exploration with people duplicating, in a more complex fashion, what we and our colleagues did four decades ago.

"A race to the moon is a dead end. While the lunar surface can be used to develop advanced technologies, it's a poor location for homesteading. It's a lifeless, barren world; its stark desolation is matched by its hostility to all living things. We should return there only as part of an internationally led coalition to test the tools and equipment we need for our ultimate destination: homesteading Mars by way of its moons."

The screen behind him filled with images of a new spacecraft. "Instead of another race to the moon, I propose a new 'unified space vision,' a plan to ensure American space leadership for the twenty-first century."

After his speech, he showed me a small booklet describing the engineering challenges of "Mars for America" and how they might be overcome. "Robotic exploration of Mars has yielded tantalizing clues about what was once a water-soaked planet," he told me. "We now know that climate change on a vast scale has reshaped its surface. With Earth undergoing its own climate evolution, human scientific outposts on Mars could help us understand these vast planetary changes. His eyes lit up. "The best way to study Mars is with the two hands, eyes, and ears of a geologist, first on a moon orbiting Mars and then on the Red Planet's surface."

His words reminded me of what President Kennedy had said

years earlier: "We choose to go to the moon . . . and do the other things, not because they are easy, but because they are hard."

"It won't be easy," I said.

"It *will* be noble," he replied.

REFLECTIONS ON RESOLUTE COURAGE

I live in a community where acts of bravery occur on a daily basis—from things we do in Afghanistan to things we do in training and in garrison. But our recognition of bravery is not wide enough. I'm thinking of the young soldier who hears, "We're looking for volunteers, we've got to send this patrol out on a route that's been IED'd three times in the last week," and he puts up his hand and says "I'm good. I'm in." We don't necessarily recognize or celebrate this kind of courage, but it's what makes us who we are and what we are today in the Canadian Forces.

—MAJOR GENERAL MIKE DAY

WHEN ALDRIN and Armstrong were waiting to lift off from the moon, they knew they were doomed unless every component and system worked flawlessly. "We had no margin for error, no second chances," Aldrin wrote. "There were no rescue plans if the liftoff failed. Nor did we have food, water or oxygen for more than a few hours." Ron Evans, the CapCom at Mission Control gave them final instructions: "Roger, *Eagle* . . . you're cleared for takeoff." Aldrin waited a beat and said quietly, "Roger. Understand. We're number one on the runway."

"Cowardice," Lord Moran states, "is a label we reserve for something a man does. What passes through his mind is his own affair." All great leaders have a first-hand knowledge of fear and know how to cope with it. They're familiar with the fear of failure, the fear of letting the team down, and the fear of injury or loss of life. Excellence in training is the primary way they combat these dark shadows. Strategic humour, tempered to the risk at hand, is another. With time and experience, resolute courage, the capacity to stay the course in dangerous times, becomes part of their DNA.

Resolute courage is long-duration tenacity for a task even when you know you may not obtain the desired result. You do it because you want to feel comfortable looking at yourself in the mirror. You do it because it's your duty.

Courage is knowing what to fear.

— PLATO

Leadership is all about psychology. You've got to know all the hard stuff, engineering, physics, computer science and design, but you've got to know the soft stuff—the hopes, fears, ambitions, and latent courage inside you and the people in front of you, waiting for direction.

Be careful how you assess your courage. Do not base it on overconfidence in your abilities or your technologies. Do not base it on a failure to recognize the superior skill or strength of your opponents—human or natural. Base it on reality as it truly is, not as you would like it to be. As author and former foreign correspondent Chris Hedges maintains, "It takes the experience of fear and the chaos of battle, the deafening and disturbing noise, to wake us up, to make us realize that we are not who we imagined we were."

Canadian Forces in Afghanistan.

WARRIOR'S HONOUR
MASTERY OF SERVICE TO YOUR TEAM, YOUR COUNTRY, AND THE PLANET

I WAS suspended in the water beneath the ice at the geographic North Pole. Adjusting the air inside my thick neoprene suit, I made a slow 360-degree turn and gazed into the near-freezing ocean. Every direction was south. Two miles below was a submerged mountain range running from Russia to Canada. On the blue ice overhead was the blurred shadow of our tent camp and four men standing at the edge of the dive hole.

Their multidisciplinary skills included biology, geology, photography, and advanced diving. They were young, but they knew the exacting demands of what we were attempting and the consequences of failure.

It had taken five years to get here. The journey had begun in 1970 with my first expedition to Resolute Bay on Cornwallis Island five hundred miles north of the Arctic Circle. Four of us, including a marine biologist and marine geologist, made twenty-five dives beneath the broken summer ice. The next winter, I returned to the same bay with ten scientists and engineers. The temperature was thirty below zero and the sun a faint glow on the southern horizon. Protected by a small hut built on the ice, we made forty research dives with state-of-the-art diving suits and breathing systems.

The following year, I chose the month of December for my third expedition. We went back to Resolute Bay to test ourselves against days of unending darkness and searing cold. Twenty of us working in teams cut a big hole through the ice, lowered eight ballast trays to the seabed, and stacked them with nine tons of ballast. On top of this we bolted together two eight-foot transparent hemispheres with an entrance hatch. Sub Igloo — the world's first manned polar station — was our refuge and observation post for fifty more dives.

The preparation for this latest mission had taken fifteen months. Supported by the Department of National Defence and the Ministry of Science, I invited forty-five scientists, engineers, and university students to spend two months in Resolute Bay. We would carry out the first saturation dive — a twenty-four-hour stay beneath the ice — and the first oxy-helium dives in polar waters. We would conduct a first-ever oil-under-the-ice study and the first live television broadcast from beneath the sea.

One of our studies revealed that oil could penetrate sea ice from below and accelerate the melting on the surface. Another study of sea-floor sediments found evidence of chemical defoliants used in far-off Vietnam during the twenty-year war.

Our most challenging project was to make the first science dives under the ice at the North Pole. Five of us boarded a C-130 Hercules in Resolute Bay and flew to Alert, the Canadian Forces base on the north coast of Ellesmere Island. At this bleak outpost on the edge of the Arctic Ocean, Lieutenant Colonel John Dardier briefed us on a military exercise called Operation Frozen Tusker.

Every month hundreds of commercial jets flew over the frozen ocean between Europe and North America. If a disabled aircraft were forced to land on the ice the Canadian Forces would fly out to recover the survivors. With more than one hundred participants, Operation Frozen Tusker was a full-scale search-and-rescue training mission.

Then two Hercules aircraft and a pair of CH-113 helicopters

lifted off from the Canadian Forces base at Alert on Ellesmere Island, flew us across four hundred miles of Arctic Ocean and set us down at the North Pole. A seven-man para-rescue team led by Lieutenant Colonel Dardier parachuted out of one of the Hercules. As Dardier and his men headed back to Alert, we set up camp and began cutting our dive hole through the ice. Three days from now, we would be "rescued."

In the sunlit water under the polar ice, I took a small Canadian flag attached to an aluminum pole, turned it upside down, drove the sharp tip of the pole up into the ice and watched the red maple leaf slowly unfurl in the water.

It took the skill and determination of hundreds of people to put the flag in place. Visionary leaders in Ottawa saw that first-ever science dives at the North Pole added meaning to a military exercise. Canadian Forces planners did the complex thinking that led to a robust conceptual plan. Military engineers and mechanics worked around the clock to ensure the aircraft were flight-ready. Canadian Forces pilots assessed the weather and sea ice, made precision fuel drops, and flew their helicopters and Hercules aircraft outside the envelope to make sure we landed at the Pole.

Working inside this military enterprise gave me a new understanding of honour. Some of the pilots had answered their nation's call and flown through the fire of war. They'd seen comrades killed and wounded. For them, warrior's honour, a special blend of honesty, integrity, and ethics, was a central value. They had a sense of responsibility to each other and their nation that most Canadians had never experienced.

It was evident in the off-the-cuff, unrehearsed things they did. The way they asked questions about the dives you were planning to make under the ice. Their confidence in you to make the scheduled radio calls to the base in Alert. The unspoken message was that if you kept your end of the bargain they would take care of you and bring you home safely. There were moments when their rigorously spare words had the mark of nobility.

VAIL, COLORADO. High mountains. Thick stands of big trees. Snow that never stops falling.

The first thing you notice is his black Stetson with the Seventh Cavalry insignia, gold braid, and three stars above its wide brim. Then you are drawn to his eyes—burning, blue eyes that have seen slaughter beyond endurance.

I was in Vail at the Strong Round Table on Leadership talking to Lieutenant General Hal Moore. I wasn't saying much, just listening intently as he recited lines from Kipling's "The Young British Soldier." "'When the half-made recruit goes out to the East, he acts like a babe and drinks like a beast . . .'"

A graduate of the US Military Academy at West Point, Moore led his troops into the first major battle of the Vietnam War. In November 1965, in the steep-sloped, jungle-covered Ia Drang Valley, he and his 390 men engaged in a fierce three-day firefight. Surrounded and outnumbered four to one, they fought against an enemy who would massacre a sister battalion two and a half miles away. Moore's blond hair inspired his men to call him "Yellow Hair," a tongue-in-cheek reference to General George Custer, commander of the Seventh Cavalry at the Battle of the Little Big Horn. Moore and his troops killed more than seven hundred enemy soldiers, lost seventy-nine of their own, and fought their way out of the area. For many, the battle became a microcosm of the war.

Before the fight, Moore spoke to his men. "We're moving into the valley of the shadow of death, where you will watch the back of the man next to you, as he will watch yours . . . I can't promise

I will bring you all home alive, but this I swear: When we go into battle, I will be the first one to set foot on the field and I will be the last to step off. And I will leave no one behind. Dead or alive, we will come home together."

The man sitting beside me was eighty-nine years old. In constant pain because of injuries from a helicopter crash and parachuting mishaps, he used a cane and occasionally a wheelchair. But Moore was once a young soldier. He knew the years when youth was a magical power with which you could accomplish anything. His voice was hoarse and hesitant, but his face with its crooked smile and sharp, significant nose was tight with resolution.

Since retirement Moore had become an ardent spokesperson for personal and professional leadership. He'd given hundreds of speeches to corporations, universities, and high school students. Three years ago, in his hometown of Auburn, Alabama, he established the National Youth Leadership Academy. Among his favourite leadership precepts were these:

A leader must be visible and exhibit confidence under any set of circumstances; the determination to prevail must be felt by all.

In your study of history and leadership qualities, pay special attention to why leaders fail.

Never deprive a person of his or her self-respect. Great leaders learn to lead themselves first; before you can lead others you must lead yourself successfully every day.

When you're up against a tough problem, never quit. There's always one more thing you can do to influence any situation in your favour.

"I saw a lot of battles in two wars," he told me. "I remember dragging the wounded into aid stations and they were lying on the ground screaming in pain."

Moore knew that at that moment, as we talked, a battle was going on somewhere, and its commanders were facing fear and exhaustion. He had devoted his life to helping young leaders find candour, competence, commitment, and courage. For him, leadership was luminous. He had that special quality lazy men will never know—an understanding, a grace, an elevation of spirit, that comes from hard work, sacrifice, and suffering.

REFLECTIONS ON WARRIOR'S HONOUR

IN BATTLE, leaders face their greatest challenge. The work is hazardous, threats are unpredictable, stress is severe, and conditions are arduous. In no other field of action does the leader make decisions based on less reliable information.

Because battle dangers are so great, everyone must be ready at a moment's notice to assume leadership. This is why the study of military leadership begins on the first day of basic training and continues as long as the soldier remains in the ranks. The rules are simple: Military leaders must be wiser and braver than those they lead. They must communicate clearly and exercise discipline. Above all, they must display integrity. The renowned Greek warrior Xenophon wrote these rules in 300 B.C. The military has practised them for more than two thousand years.

Warrior's honour—the mastery of service to your team, your country, and the planet—is a form of unconditional commitment and trust. Like love. "Love is not a word that military leaders throw around easily," says Hal Moore, "but it is the truth, as I know it—especially if you are a military leader."

I'd seen a version of warrior's honour on the navy ship during the search for the USS *Scorpion*, and with Captain Bond and his navy divers, but because I'd never been in combat—that chaos of raw brutality and monstrous fear—I didn't know the feeling of it under my ribcage. It was something I might never know. But at the top of the world with ice in every direction, and at a military base in Afghanistan, I was proud to be in the company of men and women who understood its subtle dimensions.

Men and women who serve in uniform, or as astronauts or on deep-sea science teams, have certain things in common. They focus on professional competence. They are committed to do whatever it takes to get the job done. They look after each other and adapt to change. Their ethos is in the phrase "duty with honour." Duty is why they serve; honour is how they serve.

Great leaders operate within a framework of deeply held values about life and how to live it. They study literature, psychology, philosophy, and sociology to understand the hopes, fears, aspirations, and dilemmas of humanity. Knowing the extraordinary outline of the human story and the essential issues our ancestors struggled for brings them wisdom, humility, and hard-won personal beliefs.

> Anyone can become angry—that is easy. But to be angry with the right person, to the right degree, at the right time, for the right purpose, and in the right way—this is not easy.
>
> —ARISTOTLE

> I learned about leadership in basic training. It's centered on honesty, integrity, loyalty and obedience. Honesty goes without question. Integrity is continued self-control. Loyalty goes down to the men and women whose lives you're responsible for. Obedience is your duty upwards. The acronym is HI-LO. Honesty. Integrity. Loyalty. Obedience. I try to live that every day.
>
> —LIEUTENANT COLONEL CONRAD MALKOWSKI

I'm going to close this section with a story—for three reasons. First, to confirm that women fill the ranks of deep leaders as competently and as gallantly as men. Second, because it refers to "mentoring" and will prepare you for the next section. And finally, because the shuttle astronaut Megan McArthur is one of those very special people who ride rockets for a living and make the rest of us wish we could perform our own tasks with equal grace.

SHE WAS inside the space shuttle's crew cabin, in front of the aft control panel, looking through the payload bay window at the eleven-ton satellite. Her long black hair was floating freely behind her head. As big as a school bus and gleaming silver in the sunlight, the satellite was moving at the same speed as the shuttle.

Using the translational hand controller, she slowly reached out with the fifty-foot, six-jointed robotic arm, seized a pin on the side of the billion-dollar satellite, locked into it, and gently eased the satellite toward a berthing mechanism at the back of the payload bay. If she'd had time to look, she would have seen the Atlantic Ocean and the west coast of Africa more than three hundred miles below.

"Houston, *Atlantis*, Hubble has arrived on board," said the shuttle's commander, Scott Altman.

"I'd trained for all kinds of things to go wrong," Megan McArthur told me after her thirteen-day mission, "But when I reached out to grab it, everything happened like it was supposed to. I felt calm, so calm. The video we took shows me with a big grin on my face. It was a great feeling."

The slim, steel rod of a woman earned that grin. Shortly after Hubble was launched (with astronaut Kathy Sullivan inside her spacesuit as it floated out of the payload bay) it was discovered that its primary mirror had been polished to the wrong shape. Three years later, astronauts installed corrective optics, the heavens snapped into focus, and astronomy changed forever. During its nineteen years in space, the telescope circled the earth 97,000 times, giving thousands of astronomers access to the stars from outside Earth's atmosphere and delivering a blizzard of breathtaking images. One showed a luminous object emitting light when the universe was in its infancy, 13 billion years ago.

The cylindrical satellite with two twenty-five-foot solar panels had been repaired four times. On this final mission the astronauts' objective was to install two new instruments, bring two ailing ones back to life, and replace the gyroscopes and batteries. If successful, the earth-orbiting observatory would be good for five more years.

I met McArthur on a research ship in the North Atlantic. She was one of two NASA scientists participating in Jim Cameron's *Aliens of the Deep* expedition. The smiling thirty-two-year old with green eyes was an expert in underwater acoustic propagation and digital signal processing and had served as chief scientist on several oceanographic expeditions. Although softspoken, she radiated curiosity, energy, and discipline. Three years earlier, NASA selected her as a mission specialist. After twenty-four months of training she was assigned to the Astronaut Office Shuttle Operations Branch where she served as the crew support astronaut for the Expedition 9 crew during their six-month mission aboard the International Space Station.

McArthur was right at home watching Cameron's team use four subs to explore the mountain range running down the centre of the Atlantic Ocean. When she was studying aerospace engineering at the University of California, she and five fellow students built a small, two-person sub. She learned to scuba dive and became its pilot. In graduate school at the Scripps Institution of Oceanography she studied applied ocean sciences—"oceanography for engineers." Cameron's expedition was the first time she'd seen the eighteen-ton, teardrop-shaped *Mirs*, and they gave her a new appreciation for the forces at play in the deep ocean.

"The astronauts who'd flown before—Scott Altman, Greg Johnson, and John Grunsfeld—were wonderful in-flight mentors," she told me. "They showed me how to get things done in space. I'd trained for technical tasks like operating the arm, but couldn't train for the micro-gravity things like where to put my spoon or sleeping bag. They readily shared their knowledge; they were quick with their insights."

John Grunsfeld was leading his third Hubble service mission. During his first, on one of the longest spacewalks to date, he replaced four gyroscopes. Three years later, he replaced thirty-four tightly packed connectors in a power control unit. This time, "the Hubble repairman" and his crewmates fixed the advanced camera for surveys and a spectrograph named STIS. He slipped inside the telescope, removed hundreds of tiny screws, replaced circuit cards, and reinserted the screws. The spectrograph had one card; the camera had four. The work on the camera was done around a corner behind a strut. This weightless "brain surgery in a blind area" was performed with ultra-sensitive oven-mitt gloves.

What made Grunsfeld such a splendid mentor was that he was a blue-ribbon astronomer as well as an astronaut. He knew the scientific impact of "the most important astronomical instrument ever created." Grunsfeld was one of those mentors you pray for when you want to understand the significance of your task.

Looking like a cylindrical silver snowman with white paddle arms, "Mr. Hubble" spent six days in the far end of the payload bay undergoing an overhaul. During each of the five spacewalks, McArthur took up her position on the flight deck's aft work panel and operated the robotic arm. "A crew member was always on the end of the arm. My job was to move them around so they could work hands free.

"The biggest challenge was that there were things I couldn't see out the window or on the video monitors. As I moved the crew member from the payload bay to the telescope and back again, he talked me around the solid structures. Our communication was clear and concise, something I learned as a CapCom in Mission Control. The last thing I wanted to do was to nudge the telescope."

During the five spacewalks, white-suited astronauts working in claustrophobic conditions contended with frozen bolts, stripped screws, and stuck handrails. A few hours after Hubble was buttoned up for the last time, McArthur reached out with the robotic arm, gently seized the telescope on its berthing mechanism, and lifted it free. With the hard blue curve of the earth moving slowly beneath her, she raised it clear of the payload bay and released it. Commander Altman backed the shuttle away and dropped down to a lower orbit. Far above them, the wrinkled silver icon of cosmic exploration was ready to perform more groundbreaking science.

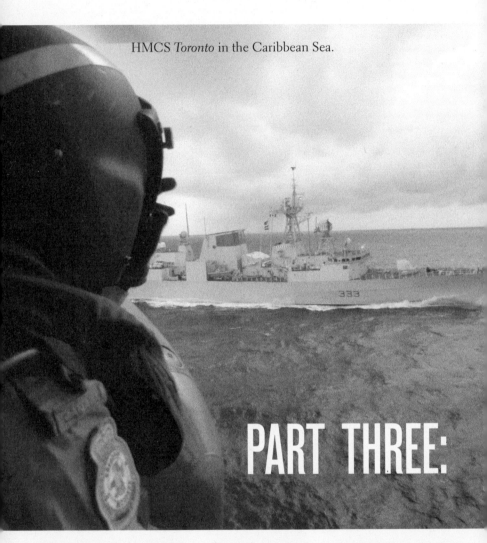

HMCS *Toronto* in the Caribbean Sea.

PART THREE:

NAVIGATING TOWARD LEADERSHIP

SOME OF you are thinking, "It's wonderful you've had these magic moments with high achievers who work in lethal environments but I'm not sure how your insights apply to me.

Here's how.

The first thing to understand is that you already possess leadership traits. You don't call them by the same names but you have your own version of cool competence, strategic imagination, fierce ingenuity, physical robustness, and some of the others. My stories about high achievers are to get you thinking about the components of leadership you already have and how you can improve and add to them.

Keep in mind that the twelve "essential" traits are not the definitive list; it is just my list. In this section I'm going to encourage you to create your own.

There's something else I should add. I'm not sure that leadership is driven primarily by intelligence. I believe it's driven mostly by empathy and enthusiasm. Empathy for the team, the task, and the technology, and a sustained enthusiasm for whatever it takes to get the job done.

I say this with some authority because by any academic measurement I don't have a hot-flame intelligence. I was a child who studied what interested him and ignored what didn't. My formal education was a long trek through high school and university prodded by patient teachers who loved their craft and long stretches of flank-speed memorizing. Each year when the marks were posted, I was consistently anchored in the bottom ten percent of the class. I'm academically challenged, largely self-taught, and a huge believer in the alchemy of self-education.

Genetically, I'm blessed with some strong cards. I have an endless curiosity about the natural world, the mechanical world, the human family and the shifting boundaries where they interact. I want to know how to read situations and discern underlying patterns. I want to know how to build trusting relationships, imagine alternative futures, and correct my own shortcomings.

For reasons I still don't comprehend, I have a lot of energy and a strong desire to know more about people who take risks to understand how the world works. I've also had more than my share of good fortune; I've been in the right place at the right time when a charismatic challenge and an alpha leader came along. These strong cards have allowed me to hide my intellectual shortcomings behind the bright fire of enthusiasm.

Just to confirm what you already know: this is not a science book written by a scientist about leadership. It's a series of observations from an accidental leader of average intelligence. It's a field guide on a subject that has an infinite number of practitioners operating on many levels.

One of those levels has to do with the "quick-change" roles required of leaders in rapidly shifting situations. One minute a leader is "the defender," solving a security crisis with confidence and strength. A few minutes later she's "the persuader," motivating her group to navigate its way through obstacles and setbacks. Then she becomes the "team builder," negotiating agreements between rival ideas and colliding egos. Without pausing she switches to "the innovator" and comes up with new ideas and spaces for breakthroughs to flourish. When a member of the team is going through a tough time she becomes "the nurturer" who extends sympathy and understanding.

Leadership is all about fulfilling the "needs" of the group and the individuals within the group. American psychologist Abraham Maslow artfully projected these needs as a pyramid, in which basic needs had to be met before you moved on to other needs. The pyramid's lowest level has the primal needs of food, water, sex, and sleep. The next level has the need for security, order, and stability. The third level—love and belonging—is about family, friendships, and social relationships. The layer above it has the needs for confidence, achievement, and respect by others. At the peak of the pyramid are problem solving, creativity, and morality.

The four levels can be summarized as: Safety and Security; Friendships and Relationships; Achievement and Success; Creativity and Morality. Each one of us has these unspoken needs and so do the teams we lead. Good leaders are constantly aware of them and searching for the best ways to satisfy them.

IN THIS section I'm going to try to convince you that leadership is like love. There is no formula for it. The yearning for it gets you up in the morning and keeps you awake at night. You continually assess and reassess what you say and how you say it. You constantly examine your leadership traits and amp up the weak ones. You navigate through uncertainty by mimicking actions from this person, adding ideas from that book, and stir-frying them with hard-won lessons learned from recent events. You hold fast to your core values. You learn that the art of influencing people is a continuously evolving process. As the combat soldiers in Afghanistan told me, "Leadership is a mission that never ends."

I'm also going to try to convince you that although there are no rules for becoming a leader or maintaining strong leadership, there are steps to help you begin and sustain the journey.

The first is commitment. You have to believe that leadership is an indispensable skill and be determined to develop it.

The second step is to command the language. To command the moment, you have to command the language.

The third step is to recognize that books and films contain important insights about leadership. You slowly build a leadership library.

The fourth step is to find men and women willing to mentor you in the art of leadership.

The final step is to seek leadership opportunities and measure your progress honestly. Your objective is to develop a continually emerging, transformative character.

Mercury space capsule *Aurora 7*.

MAKING THE COMMITMENT

IF YOU listen to an astronaut talk about her upcoming mission, see a special ops commander describe his next assignment (or watch Larry Page describe Google's new initiative) you're witnessing leadership "commitment." Sometimes it's so palpable it makes the air hum. Part determination, part discipline, and part vision, commitment is the starting point of every challenge including leadership.

All the leaders I've read about or interviewed start their journey by asking fundamental questions. What is my purpose in life and what are my unique skills? Who are my heroes in history and real life? What qualities do I admire in myself? What are the qualities I look for in friends and mentors? To create a solid starting point in your leadership journey you must ask the same questions about yourself and write them down.

As time passes, you will revisit and revise this list. It is your personal mission statement.

Among the first commitments you make is to honestly assess your own traits and decide what's hot and what's not. How cool is your competence? How high is your empathy? When your deadline-driven project hits the boiling point will you have the strength and stamina to combat the stress? Using my twelve traits as your starting point, write out a list of your own and give them compelling names.

Keep in mind that as an apprentice leader you don't need all twelve traits. Many leader-managers motor along on four or five. They have vision and are good communicators; they empathize with to the needs of their team. The secret is to assess the traits you have and the traits you see in other people.

Over the years my leadership performance has gone through peaks and valleys. There were times when I really clicked with my teams and we achieved some tough objectives. There were moments when I displayed too much authority and too little empathy. Too often I was swept up in purpose, plans, and people with not enough time for reflection. Too often being a testosterone-driven male blinded me to some pretty obvious flaws.

Looking back, these are the marks I would give myself:

Cool Competence:	B
Powerful Presentations:	B+
Physical Toughness:	C
Mental Resilience:	B
Strategic Imagination:	C
High-Empathy Communication:	B+
Hot-Zone Humour:	C+
Blood Trust	B
Fierce Ingenuity:	C
Team Genius:	C
Resolute Courage:	C
Warrior's Honour:	C

In summary, I'm pretty good at giving keynote speeches but you better not count on me to solve your high-tech problems. When it comes to computers and software, I'm someone who thinks a megabyte is something made by a great white shark.

Once you've made a list of your essential traits you can use them to assess the leaders you encounter every day. How good is your boss at communicating his vision to the members of your team? How well does she master levity and laughter to reduce code-red moments? What's the track record on high-risk, long-duration decisions of the politician you're thinking of voting for?

Pierre Trudeau was deeply committed to a set of values centred on human rights and social justice. You could argue with his politics, but you had to acknowledge his profound commitment to high-risk, long-duration decisions. Here's an example.

A few months after we built the first polar research station under the Arctic Ocean, I was invited to have lunch with him at 24 Sussex Drive. I stopped at the gate, passed the hard scrutiny of two Royal Canadian Mounted Policemen, and parked my car. A few minutes later I was ushered into the dining room. Trudeau and another man were sitting at a small table overlooking the wind-blurred Ottawa River. He introduced me to Aleksandr Yakovlev, a Russian historian and the new Soviet ambassador to Canada. Yakovlev was in his mid-fifties and wore a black suit. He had a round face, thick eyebrows, and a high, bald forehead. I sensed that if he felt the need he would cut through you like a chainsaw.

For the next hour we talked about the five-million-square-mile Arctic Ocean shared by both nations. It was clear I was in the company of two highly attentive men. I could sense them listening and analyzing with reason and intuition.

At one point, Trudeau asked me to describe how we constructed the station on the floor of the ocean. As I told my story, Yakovlev furrowed his brows and leaned forward. I could feel him trying to understand the implications of a small observation post in an ocean being used by Soviet and American navies to hide ballistic missile nuclear submarines.

The two men talked briefly about the arms race. Trudeau was deeply concerned about the mass incineration and radioactive fallout of nuclear weapons. Eleven years earlier he had written in *Cité Libre*: "Twisted, charred, liquefied, volatilized . . . there will remain only traces of (human) shadows imprinted on the concrete debris, on stones in the fields, on cliffs overlooking the sea." Much of his political energy, including his drive toward rapprochement with Russia, was devoted to reducing—if possible, eliminating—the threat of nuclear war. A master practitioner of the politics of inclusion, he used scientific exchanges, trade, tourism, and culture as weapons of peace.

A few years after my lunch with the prime minister, Mikhail Gorbachev was elected General Secretary of the Politburo of the Soviet Union. One of his principal advisors was Aleksandr Yakovlev. Both men were committed to changing the governance and economy of their country. At Yakovlev's urging, Gorbachev introduced *glasnost* ("openness"), *perestroika* ("restructuring"), and *demokratizatsiya* ("democratization"). There was hardline resistance from party bureaucrats, but Gorbachev and Yakovlev persisted, knowing that if reforms didn't come from above they would come from below and tear the Soviet Union apart.

In the summer of 1989 Gorbachev initiated events that marked the beginning of the end of the Cold War. As Communist regimes in Poland, Hungary, Czechoslovakia, and East Germany fell, he agreed to a phased and peaceful withdrawal of Soviet troops. A year later, these strategically imagined steps earned him the Nobel Peace Prize.

Trudeau's own commitment to nuclear disarmament and peace among nations never wavered. In late 1983 he travelled to China, Washington, East Germany, and the Soviet Union, and urged political leaders to consider the reduction of nuclear weapons, a non-proliferation treaty, and a ban on high-altitude anti-satellite missiles. Less than a year after Trudeau's "peace mission," President Reagan echoed one of its basic principles: "nuclear war cannot be won and must never be fought." Six years later, the Berlin Wall was torn down.

In the long, uphill struggles as leaders of their countries, Trudeau and Gorbachev took many significant steps. One of the most important was their commitment to high-risk leadership. Another was to learn how to command the language, a subject we'll explore in the next section.

REFLECTIONS ON MAKING THE COMMITMENT

YOU CAN choose to be a leader, with your family, your community, or your nation, at any time. Focus your energy on the job at hand and don't be concerned about your future prospects. The key is a commitment to the mission and your team.

> Are you in earnest? Seize this very minute!
> What you can do—or dream you can—begin it!
> Courage has genius, power and magic in it.
> —GOETHE

When they are young, aspiring leaders are captivated by stories about historically important people. Later in life, they're inspired by the ideas and actions of the living—their contemporaries. They make a commitment to understanding why these men and women are successful at influencing other people. They try to determine the qualities of a good leader. They begin the hard task of developing these qualities in themselves.

> You make a habit of studying people, finding out the way they talk, the answers they give and their points of view; then you reflect on what's on their faces and how they act because most people like to see reflections of themselves. If you want something from an audience, you give blood to their fantasies.
> —MARLON BRANDO

"I have long been accustomed . . . ," wrote President Teddy Roosevelt, to ". . . doing the best I was able to do in a position I did not altogether like, and under conditions I didn't like at all."

In spite of being lifelong Communists, Yakovlev and Gorbachev were ardently committed to changing their societies. It was visible in the way they spoke and the way they carried themselves. They endured risks and suffered censure. For them, commitment to leadership was everything.

> It's never too late to be what you want to be. There's no time limit. Start whenever you want. You can change or stay the same. There are no rules to this thing. You can make the best or the worst of it. I hope you make the best of it. I hope you see things that startle you. I hope you feel things you never felt before. I hope you meet people who have a different point of view. I hope you live a life you're proud of, and if you're not, I hope you have the courage to start all over again.
> —ERIC ROTH

In spite of its psychological (and occasionally, financial) benefits, leadership is hard and lonely work. You're surrounded by ardent admirers and determined detractors. Many people tell you what they think you want to hear. The information coming from all sources is often inadequate. You're navigating through a fog and at the darkest moments, you're navigating alone.

> Leadership is the most crucial choice one can make—it is the decision to step out of the darkness into the light.
> —DEEPAK CHOPRA

Almost everything—all external expectations, all pride, all fear of embarrassment or failure—these things just fall away in the face of death, leaving only what is truly important. Remembering that you are going to die is the best way I know to avoid the trap of thinking you have something to lose. You are already naked. There is no reason not to follow your heart.

—STEVE JOBS

Commander Richard Feltham on HMCS *Toronto*.

COMMANDING THE LANGUAGE

ABOUT THE same time I was starting my struggles in the classroom, I was discovering the power of words. I grew up in an upstairs duplex that had six bookcases holding classic and contemporary novels, art books, and rows of fascinating non-fiction. My older brother and I watched our single mom light up a cigarette, open a cold beer, and read a book as she watched us play. She always had a book on the go, its pages turned slowly as she devoured its contents.

I copied her. I leafed through art and travel books. I thumbed through *Life, Look,* and *National Geographic.* Slowly, wonderfully, a universe of images and possibilities opened up. I didn't have to understand every word; the pictures carried much of the story.

I started a journal and scribbled melancholy schoolboy thoughts. In high school I had some of those glorious teachers I mentioned earlier—men and women passionate about literature, eager to have their students follow them through the pathways of grammar, punctuation, short stories, and Charles Dickens. The best of them encouraged me to write.

I was on to something but didn't know exactly what it was. My first two years in university offered some insight; my only A in a forest of Cs was in English literature. When I started working for Ed Link I discovered that good writing could accelerate my career. Putting ideas on paper forced me to think with precision, and plan ahead. This discipline would soon help me to speak clearly in front of small groups of people.

I worked hard at constructing convincing letters and reports. Well-written sentences and paragraphs became an obsession. These literary "smart bombs" allowed me to convince my bosses to start new projects and spend time with other scientists in my field. They opened the door to my first major magazine article for *Scientific American*. A collateral benefit was that people began to think I was more intelligent than I was.

I developed a formula that made me a better writer. I call it ABC squared. A is for Accuracy. Write with pinpoint accuracy or the truth police will come calling. B is for Brevity. Work hard to eliminate the padding and dog poop. C is for Clarity. Keep things kindergarten simple. The "squared" is a reminder to add sparkle, mystery, and humour or as the acclaimed writer Peter C. Newman says, "Make the facts dance."

Over the years, writing has been the main engine of my personal and professional leadership. I've written magazine articles on issues of ocean conservation and hammered out proposals for Arctic research and The Friends of the Environment Foundation. I've penned scientific summaries and technical reports for the Canadian government and large corporations. I've written hundreds of keynote speeches. This book is part of that evolving continuum.

Good writing is a contact sport. Every time I write a news article, a book outline, a letter of apology, or a keynote speech I take it as an opportunity to improve my style. You can do the same. Your objective is to make your words stand out from the torrent.

I've had the good fortune to work with some outstanding writing mentors. One of the first was the short, stocky editor at

Scientific American who red-pencilled my first draft and passed along his paraphrased words of D.H. Lawrence: "When you've got nothing to say shut up. When genuine passion moves you, say what you've got to say, and say it hot."

I met Peter C. Newman when he was transforming *Maclean's* into Canada's national weekly newsmagazine. The tall, soft-spoken journalist was my "writer-hero" because he fused the hardheaded rules of journalism with the art of creative writing and "made the facts dance." His unique ability with words made him the most influential Canadian journalist of his generation.

Like all good mentors Newman was happy to share his hard-won wisdom. I remember talking to him about the value of good stories. "Robert Fulford said it best," he told me. "Stories are how we explain, how we teach, how we entertain ourselves and how we often do all three at once. They are the juncture where facts and feelings meet."

Newman was patient with my endless questions about how to become a better writer.

"Read hard. Write about what you know. Write every day. Above all *be original*."

Newman writes with the music of Stan Kenton pulsating through his ears. "Pay attention to cadence," is one of his mantras. "Select words and rhythms that appeal to the reader's inner ear. Make your sentences sing."

WHEN I worked on ocean policy in Ottawa I met dozens of dedicated scientists, engineering experts, and creative artists. I soon discovered that men and women in these disciplines are indirect leaders; they influence others primarily through the sustained merit of their work.

As the ocean policy came together I spent time around the table with senior members of the civil service. Like politicians and corporate leaders, they are direct leaders. They lead through their actions and stories.

The best political and corporate leaders know that "the story" is central. It has to be timed for the historical moment and be strong enough to supplant earlier stories and counter-stories. In the constant Darwinian competition among narratives, only the most robust survive.

From a small desk in the Privy Council Office, I watched government officials craft the story that would best engage the group they were trying to influence. If it was a big story for a large audience, they frequently shaped it as a drama, a "heroic" journey unfolding over time: where we've come, where we're headed, and what we should struggle against and dream about.

After my third Arctic research expedition, I was asked to write an article for *National Geographic* magazine. In Washington, in the white marble building on M Street, the expeditions editor, Bill Graves, pushed me hard on the importance of writing a good outline followed by an article held together with short, clear sentences. On my second visit he took me down the hallway and introduced me to a man who had written fifty-five articles for the magazine.

Bald, energetic and sporting an elegant moustache, Luis Marden was the chief of foreign staff. A photographer, writer, filmmaker, sailor, and humorous raconteur, he epitomized "the *Geographic* man," the old-time writer-adventurer who travelled the globe searching for new and exciting stories. One of his specialties was undersea exploration. After weeks of diving in the dangerous Pacific swells off Pitcairn Island in the South Pacific and ignoring an islander's grim prophecy—"Man, you gwen be dead as a hatchet!"—Marden discovered the remains of the fabled ship *Bounty*. The news made headlines around the world.

The High Arctic was one of the few places on the planet Marden had not visited and he wanted to know more about how we survived the near-freezing temperatures beneath the ice. In time we became good friends and occasionally he invited me to stay with him and his wife Ethel in their Frank Lloyd Wright house overlooking the Potomac River in Virginia.

Marden was my gold standard when it came to mentorship in writing. His manners and bearing were courtly and his humour was self-deflating. He introduced me to the interplay between speaking and writing. Write the way you talk, he told me. Write simply, clearly, and without repetition and clichés. Learn to recite poetry and quote prose.

Marden's small office at the *Geographic* was wall-to-wall with books and photographs. There were dictionaries in Latin, Spanish, French, and Arabic, and thick volumes on sailboats, orchids, and birds. There were signed photographs of the King of Tonga and Orville Wright. I remember thinking: if this is what "self-taught" can do, I have to get busy.

Marden was obsessed with facts and details. He taught himself five languages and was working on several others. He was cited six times in Webster's dictionary for words such as "snick" and "sevillana." He also had a built-in bullshark detector. "I wouldn't trust anything that used me as a source," he once told me.

Marden inspired a generation of writers and photographers at *National Geographic*. In every sentence or turn of phrase he demonstrated what a storyteller could be. A leader. A teacher. A friend. "Your mind is a palace," he was fond of saying. "So build a king's library for all of its rooms."

In the next section we'll look at how assembling a library of physical and virtual books can help make you a better leader.

REFLECTIONS ON COMMANDING THE LANGUAGE

GOOD WRITING, with accuracy, brevity, and clarity, is a fountainhead leadership skill. Writing forces you to understand the energy and impact of words, sentences, and paragraphs; it's the first step to becoming an eloquent public speaker. To command the moment, you must command the language.

Telling your leadership story with words is your starting point. "Stories of identity," says author and social scientist Howard Gardner, "constitute the single most powerful weapon in the leader's literary arsenal." Keep in mind that in a world where information is coming faster and faster, you are competing for your readers' time. To hold their interest you have to entertain as well as inform, in sentences that hot-wire emotions to intellect. In a social-media-and-image-driven world you must consider how to use still and moving pictures to enhance your words. Today we don't just *tell* stories, we *relate* them.

> Writing is an affair of yearning for great voyages and hauling on frayed ropes.
> —ISRAEL SHENKER

> So, this above all: Find your own voice.
> —CHRISTOPHER HITCHENS

> I love all men who dive. Any fish can swim near the surface, but it takes a great whale to go downstairs five miles or more . . . I'm not talking about Mr. Emerson now—but that whole corps of thought-divers that have been diving and coming up again with blood-shot eyes since the world began.
>
> — HERMAN MELVILLE

US Navy captain George Bond wrote every day. He wrote steadily, carefully, reflecting on his colleagues, his divers, and the risky experiments they were engaged in. He told me his ability to get his teams to believe they could do great things was born on the pages of his journal.

Bond was a powerful public speaker who used the natural resonance of his voice to hold the audience's attention. He would slow for effect, pause at just the right moment or let his words trail off to emphasize a point. He used his knowledge of literature to master dynamic images and anecdotes. "Every speech I made," he told me, "started with the notes in my journal."

Writing enlarges the terrain of knowledge inside your head. Writing lets you see your thoughts in real time.

Your language expresses your character. It has traces of the family you grew up in, the schools you went to, the books you have read, the jobs you have held, and the people you associate with. It gives the listener insight to your memories, dreams, and ambitions, and your politics, prejudices, and philosophy. Be creative: the way you form sentences indicates your outlook on life; the way you use words reveals your mood and aspirations.

> A page of good prose remains invincible.
>
> — JOHN CHEEVER

The difference between the right word and the almost right word is the difference between lightning and the lightning bug.

— MARK TWAIN

Megan McArthur inside the space shuttle.

BUILDING A LIBRARY

IN MY third year in high school I began using my pocket money to buy books. At first I purchased them because I was enchanted with the characters in novels like *Lord Jim* and *A Tale of Two Cities* and wanted easy access to their thoughts and deeds. Then, driven by curiosity about how the world works, I started buying science books. My interests ranged from physiology to geology to astrobiology. In university, realizing how desperately little I knew about the humanities, I brought home all twenty-one volumes in the Great Book series. Collecting became an unruly passion. On a trip to London, I found a set of Joseph Conrad's first editions in a small bookshop. By my late thirties I was a full-blown bookaholic. It's only fair to warn you that the following thoughts are from an addict in recovery.

If you like the shape and texture of ideas there's a good chance you already have a substantial library. It will include biographies that inspired you to overcome failure, tragedies that taught you about the perils of pride, comedies that schooled you in humour, and westerns that informed you about endurance. It will include poetry and war stories that brought a better understanding about death and bravery. It's safe to say that the best of your books contain insights about leadership.

There are hundreds of volumes on the subject. At one end of the spectrum, the message is direct and obvious. Think *Drucker on Leadership*. At the other end of the spectrum, the message is soul-whisperer subtle. Think *For Whom the Bell Tolls*. One of your challenges is to assess where you are on your leadership journey—apprentice, practitioner, or master—and select the right books to help you move forward. Here are some suggestions.

If you're a leader-to-be, Hemingway's *For Whom the Bell Tolls* is a great read. (As young men, both John McCain and Barack Obama were inspired by it.) Its central character is Robert Jordan, a young American professor fighting on the Republican side against General Franco in the Spanish Civil War. An expert in the use of explosives, Jordan makes his way into the war zone to lead a small band of guerrillas in an attack on an enemy bridge. In planning and executing the attack he repeatedly risks his life, while maintaining the highest standards of honesty, integrity, compassion, and courage. This is warrior's honour at its finest.

In his short novel *The Old Man and the Sea,* Hemingway tells the story of a Cuban fisherman who spends days in a small boat far from shore trying to land a huge tuna to feed his family. It is a magnificent description of physical robustness and mental resilience.

Daniel Goleman's *Emotional Intelligence: Why It Can Matter More Than IQ* was one of the first books in my leadership library. It outlines "a different way of being smart" and reveals the factors, including self-awareness, self-discipline, and empathy, that give ordinary people an edge over those with a higher IQ. Much to my delight, Golman pointed out that emotional intelligence matters twice as much as cognitive abilities like IQ or technical expertise.

Goleman supported his thesis by using neurobiological data coming from brain imaging technologies. He pointed out how this information allows us to understand more clearly how the emotional centres in the brain "move us to rage or to tears and how more ancient parts of the brain, which stir us to make war as well as love, are channeled for better or worse."

If you have been practising leadership for some time and want to improve your performance, *Primal Leadership: Learning How to Lead with Emotional Intelligence* is an excellent source. Goleman and his co-authors argue that emotional intelligence — being intelligent about emotions — is vital to effective leadership. They show why a leader's moods and actions have enormous impact on those they lead; they shed fresh light on how emotionally intelligent leadership arouses the passion and enthusiasm that keep people motivated. As well, they sound warnings about how toxic leadership can poison the emotional climate of a workplace.

I'm drawn to leadership books that come at the subject with verve and humour. One of them is Robert Sutton's *The No Asshole Rule*, a rousing guide to working with and surviving bullies, creeps, tyrants, tormentors, and egomaniacs. Every leader eventually has to deal with them . . . "the selfish, uncivil, mean-spirited and flat-out rude men and women" who create the toxic social friction that ruins morale, lowers productivity, and devastates a team's productivity. Sutton's survival tactics include developing calm indifference, limiting your toxic exposure, building safety pockets of support and sanity, and showing the skunks the door.

Design your leadership library according to your specific needs. To keep abreast of the role of leadership in world events, such as American politics and the "Arab Revolutions," I have a digital subscription to the *New York Times*. Its science section gives me the latest findings in a wide range of subjects from neuroscience to psychology. David Brooks writes fascinating articles on human behaviour and culture. Maureen Dowd uses diamond-tipped words to analyze the performance of politicians and celebrities from Barack Obama to Sarah Palin and Donald Trump. Every Sunday in the business section *The Corner Office* features an interview with a CEO who offers practical insights on personal and professional leadership.

My virtual library is growing much faster than my library of physical books. (This is a good thing; at the height of my addiction, my expanding bookshelves almost forced me out onto the street.) So far, my virtual library is mostly filled with articles, but e-books (including this one), are the way of the future.

My addiction was arrested by an Internet offering access to books, articles, and photographs I can store on the hard drive of my laptop computer. Every time I turn it on I'm amazed by the ways words and images can be archived and utilized inside my "silicone brain."

Sometime a book comes along, and you know right away that it belongs in your library. My interest in leadership in life-threatening environments drew me to Amanda Ripley's *The Unthinkable: Who Survives When Disaster Strikes—And Why.* It points out that nine out of ten Americans live in places where earthquakes, hurricanes, tornadoes, and terrorism are a significant risk, and everyone should know how to increase their chances of surviving the unthinkable. It answers questions that lurk in the dark corners of our minds: How will I react when I have to make a split-second choice to save my family? What will it feel like? Will I be a hero or a victim? Will my personality or anything I've ever learned really matter? Based on information from the latest brain imaging technologies and human responses to well-known disasters like 9/11, it is a compelling look at human behaviour under extreme pressure. I consider it a "leadership" book because mortal emergencies call for the best in personal and professional leadership.

The Soul of Leadership: Unlocking Your Potential for Greatness by Deepak Chopra is an "eastern" approach to leadership. Chopra contends that great leaders are created from the level of the soul. He gives seven practical steps, summarized in the acronym LEADERS: "Look and Listen. Emotional Bonding. Awareness. Doing. Empowerment. Responsibility. Synchronicity." This is an unusual and informative introduction for new leaders.

Military leadership is the fountainhead of all other forms of leadership and at some point you should explore its dynamics. Christopher Kolenda and his co-writers have assembled an excellent overview in *Leadership: The Warrior's Art*. Using historical examples from several armies and various wars including Vietnam and the Middle East, Kolanda argues that the essence of leadership is revealed conspicuously through individual actions in times of crisis. He believes that the battlefields of history provide a unique opportunity to examine the leadership phenomenon. Lieutenant General Hal Moore called it "the best book on military leadership in peace and war I've ever read."

My library contains movies as well as books. *Apollo 13* is a riveting story about a life-threatening engineering failure and how the astronauts and Mission Control worked together to bring the wounded spacecraft back to earth. *Saving Private Ryan* is about men of honour performing heroically in the horror of battle. *Braveheart* reveals the resolute courage of Lord Wallace and his Scottish clans fighting against the English. If you tune in to them, the faces, scenes, and catchphrases of films like *Invictus* and *Avatar* give insights about what it takes to be a deep leader.

Video games are a domain you may want to explore. According to Professor James Paul Gee, "Video games are the literature of the 21st century." *America's Army*, created by a West Point professor, Casey Wardynski, emphasizes teamwork, values, and responsibility. Players go through basic training and, if successful, become Green Berets. The game, which enhances the capacity to process information and detect changes in the environment, has more than two million registered users.

A major theme running through most of my books and articles on leadership is the critical importance of mentoring young leaders. It is the subject of the next chapter.

REFLECTIONS ON BUILDING A LIBRARY

Books have shaped my life on every subject from astronomy to physics to leadership. Books are a universe waiting to be explored.

— KATHY SULLIVAN

From reading of the people I admired . . . I felt a great admiration for men who were fearless and who could hold their own in the world, and I had a great desire to be like them.

— TEDDY ROOSEVELT

LEADERS NEED to know about human nature, character, and the complexities of the human family. They have to understand the forces of the natural world. Great books, from Aristotle to Shakespeare, from Tennyson to Tolstoy to Twain, are filled with useful information. Bill Gates, co-founder of Microsoft, advances his education by reading great books every day.

When you read history, literature, science, and philosophy, you absorb the experiences and judgments of others. You heighten your powers of observation and think about current events with an enlarged perspective. You more easily respond to ideas that are convincing, constructive, and consistent.

Here are some additional favourites from my leadership library. John Gardner's *On Leadership* describes the nature, tasks, and moral dimensions of leadership. Laurence Gonzales's *Deep Survival* describes the qualities a leader needs in life-threatening environments. Keith Sawyer's *Group Genius* examines the origins of collaboration and is the source of much of what I've written about team genius.

I believe we inherit a great river of knowledge, a flow of patterns coming from many sources. The information that comes from deep in the evolutionary past we call genetics. The information that comes from hundreds of years ago we call culture. The information passed along from decades ago we call family and the information offered months ago we call education. But it is all information that flows through us. The brain is adapted to the river of knowledge and exists only as a creature in that river. Our thoughts are profoundly molded by this long historic flow and none of us exists, self-made, in isolation from it.

—DAVID BROOKS

When I was in graduate school I read about historic expeditions. One book I really loved was Ernest Shackleton's *South*—a great story about overcoming obstacles and keeping a group together. When we went into quarantine before the mission I was asked to pick a movie. My choice was *Master and Commander*. It's about what a leader must do to keep a group together.

—MEGAN McARTHUR

Books guided my life from high school, and the greatest, most interesting, most provocative, funniest, smartest people who ever lived in the last 200 or 300 years wrote those books . . . I was able to associate with great minds through their books.

—ROBERT LOOMIS

Major General Mike Day
addressing his troops.

FINDING MENTORS

AS DAVID BROOKS points out, I'm the product of streams of information that came to me through my genetics, culture, family, and education. Central to this flow of facts and concepts were hundreds of men and women who were generous with their time and honest advice. As parents, teachers, coaches, counsellors, professors, friends, and shipmates, they informed me about the natural world, the mechanical world, the social world, and human emotions. They offered constructive criticism and enthusiastic encouragement. They listened to my problems and gave me guidance. Occasionally they gave me a swift kick in the butt. They were my mentors.

I still have them. Some are half my age; others I've met only briefly. They help me understand issues, overcome obstacles, and persist in the face of failure. Among them are the good people I've written about in this book, the Merck vice-president who helped me prepare for a recent speech in Paris, and the editing staff at Random House who brought this book into being.

I have been inspired by people I admire, sometimes revere, from a distance. I've never met Nelson Mandela, but because of him I have asked hard questions about human rights, justice, and community service. With role models, there is no personal contact, just graceful actions bearing a strong informing narrative.

Sometimes the advice from my mentors comes in long rambling conversations. Sometimes it arrives in a short e-mail.

Occasionally it is delivered in one axe-sharp sentence. When the pilot of a Russian research sub spends two hours describing the life-support and communication systems inside his twenty-million-dollar vehicle and then barks, "Do NOT touch that switch until I tell you," it is a high-content message.

I've spent a long time struggling to understand the meaning of good mentoring. The best mentors have a hot-running empathy mechanism and accurately understand your position and perspective. They "get" your thoughts and feelings. They make you feel acknowledged and valued.

Mentors give much more than advice. They're emotional refuelling stations, offering reassurance, a sense of safety, and the confidence to take risks. Collectively, they allow us to build up a psychic savings account or what psychologist Simon Baron-Cohen calls "an internal pot of gold." When you're overwhelmed with challenges or need to recover from setbacks you dip into this emotional reservoir.

Within the art of mentoring there are many unspoken codes. One says that mentoring—advising and teaching—is a reciprocal process. In different ways and to different degrees, the exchange of ideas and actions benefits both teacher and pupil. Another says: "You've been taught. You have a responsibility to share what you know with others."

If you enjoy the give-and-take of constructive advice you already have good mentors. They include friends who offer a candid opinion about your behaviour, teachers who amp up your mental skills, coaches who improve your physical conditioning, the boss who helps you work through a tough assignment and inspires you to new levels of understanding and performance. It's safe to say that the best of your mentors are sharing insights on leadership.

It's also safe to say that if empathy and advice are among your strengths, you in turn are mentoring people who are worthy and in need. They include the younger sibling who is attentive to your every word, the friends who seek you out in difficult times, and the colleagues with whom you share more than a beer. Without knowing it, you're probably giving advice on personal and professional leadership.

The purpose of this chapter is to get you to think consciously about the process of mentoring and improve your skills. Start by making a list of the five most influential people in your life. Write down the most important skills, concepts, or emotions they helped you with. How many of these make you a better leader? How many of these are you passing along to the next generation?

Mentoring is not always easy and sometimes takes you into emotionally charged territory. When I was the medical director of Ocean Systems our land-based research lab was in Buffalo, NY, in a grey concrete building owned by one of our parent companies, Union Carbide. In the corner of a large room, under a bank of fluorescent lights, we had a cylindrical decompression chamber embraced by high-pressure lines, compressed-gas cylinders, life-support equipment, and shelves of physiological measuring devices. Our eight-man team was under the direction of Heinz Schreiner, a brilliant mathematician and physicist who worked for Carbide.

Schreiner was one of my early professional mentors. He taught me how to craft well-written funding proposals that brought in hundreds of thousands of dollars from the Office of Naval Research. He also taught me (by example) how not to manage people. When things didn't go his way he used subtle threats and intimidation to bring us around to his way of thinking. He was the master of the rude interruption and withering look. To be fair, he wasn't a jerk all the time and we were an unruly lot who spent too much time on ships and in Key West bars.

But as the seagoing leader of the team I decided to tell the heavy, thickset Schreiner that his behaviour was affecting our morale. He was always in a better mood after lunch so I waited until he'd had his sandwich, then went to his office and told him quietly but firmly that the bite in his words was making the guys feel bad about themselves and affecting their performance. He looked shocked and angry. There were tight-lipped words from both of us interrupted by dark silences. After about ten minutes, I backed out of the room thinking that I'd just added powder to his next verbal depth charge.

A few days later he stopped me in the hallway and told me that he wasn't aware he was hurting people's feelings and thanked me for bringing it to his attention. He turned his analytical mind on the physics of his own behaviour. The personal insults stopped coming and he became more socially sensitive. Our morale went skyward and our performance with it.

There are many don't-go-there lessons to be learned from dysfunctional leaders. Imagine a hospital in Hades, its intensive care unit filled with powerful leaders recently fallen from grace. On the walls are life-sized portraits of the impeached Bill Clinton and the disgraced Eliot Spitzer. Rows of men are lying in beds, wrapped in bandages, their swollen faces bearing scars from the explosion of their personal and professional lives. John Edwards. Arnold Schwarzenegger. Anthony Wiener. Brian Mulroney. Conrad Black. Bernie Madoff. Rupert Murdoch. Tiger Woods. Dominique Strauss-Kahn. Google these names and you'll read about men in positions of power who tripped over the roadside bombs of greed, lust, lying, and cheating.

They rose to the top of their fields because of their relentless ambition and high-bandwidth intelligence. They were brought to ground by a failure of integrity and low-bandwidth empathy.

We should be as measured with our scorn as they were with their remorse. The pinnacles of wealth and power they achieved and the temptations they succumbed to are a high-octane realm we've never experienced.

But they desperately let us down. When you're wealthy, powerful, and famous you're a role model for thousands of young people emulating your words and actions. When you shatter their trust, the collateral damage is beyond imagining.

AMONG MY recent "best mentored" moments came from the men and women fighting the Taliban in Afghanistan. Some of them had just come back from a forward operating base and yet they took time to answer my questions. They were articulate, modest, and patient. They gave me the greatest of gifts: a new way of appreciating a subject of great complexity. Their brothers and sisters on board HMCS *Toronto* were equally generous with their insights. Here are the words of Petty Officer Second Class Kerry Houghton who's been working on navy ships for eighteen years.

"For me, leadership is mentoring. It's not just showing people how to do it, but showing them how to do it in their own way. My leadership skills are mothering . . . all I do is mother people. I want them to do well, I want them to do better than me. I make a huge effort to know my subordinates; currently I have twelve. And I know every one of them. I know all of their likes and dislikes. When I ask them to do anything, they jump at it because they don't want to disappoint me. I don't have to ask twice; they just do it. They trust me. They know I'll take care of them."

REFLECTIONS ON FINDING MENTORS

EVERY TIME you carefully observe a person's character or conduct, you're learning from someone. Every time you're positive, grateful, open-hearted, or angry, you are an example to someone. As John Wooden — the legendary basketball coach — says, "There is nothing that you haven't learned from someone else. The greatest learning comes from when you've selected the right mentor."

Personal mentors give us insights into the best practices for life including honesty, humility, and disciplined thinking. Professional mentors give us insights into the best work practices including motivation, focus, and management.

Mentors affect our emotional lives, elevating us into new realms of competence, empathy, and service. Through them we learn the meaning of sound judgment and deliberate actions.

Leadership means mentoring — creating challenges, expectations, and opportunities for future leaders. It means removing obstacles, unearthing talents, and releasing energy and initiative.

A mentor is a role model, a guide, a patron, and a teacher: someone in the right place at the right time to assist an emerging leader. The mentor and the emerging leader influence each other in continuous learning that includes supervision and evaluation.

You don't have to agree with your mentor. Sometimes the best learning comes from observing other people's failures, hesitations, and mistakes. Sometimes the best learning comes from someone much younger than you.

Mentor is a verb and a noun. It is something you do; it is something you are.

Any time there is a sharing of knowledge or a teaching

experience, there is a mentor. Anywhere there is an individual with life lessons to impart and an audience of one, there is a mentor.

When the National Science Foundation asked the "breakthrough" scientists what they felt was the most favourable factor in their education, the answer was almost uniformly, "association with a great, inspiring teacher."

MENTORING IS a form of leadership that never sleeps; when you are a leader you have an enduring responsibility to mentor those who are younger, worthy, and in need.

If you're the low man or woman on the totem pole, learn from those at or close to the top. Pick their brains, follow them around. They'll probably be flattered. Even today, I'm still learning from my colleagues. When I see an interview or a story that I really like, I'll watch it several times to understand what made it so good.

—KATIE COURIC

Russian diver assists in the recovery of a *Mir* sub.

SEEKING OPPORTUNITIES

LEADERSHIP BEGINS in small places, close to home. It starts in the family, in the schoolyard, and in the workplace. It is born of the affection and empathy of parents, teachers, coaches, bosses, and friends. But, later in life, when it matures and becomes complex, it is not for the faint of heart.

One of the most difficult challenges I ever faced was as the start-up leader of the seven-million-dollar IMAX Titanic expedition. It was a two-and-a-half-year marathon of uncertainty, setbacks, and obstacles. There were long periods when failure seemed certain and I considered hauling up the white flag.

I began the project with the buoyant optimism you need when you kick-start a difficult task. I'd dived to the *Titanic*, seen her magnificent ruins up close, and knew how breathtaking they would look in the giant-screen IMAX format. I'd worked with the Russians and their *Mir* research subs and was confident there was a terrific story in Anatoly Sagalevich and his team taking us two miles down to the wreck and back. I had reliable colleagues like Emory Kristof at *National Geographic*, Steve Blasco at the Bedford Institute of Oceanography, and Al Giddings, an Emmy Award–winning filmmaker, who would provide innovative scientific and technical support. And I lived in Toronto close to IMAX's head office with easy access to their senior management. In summary, I had a clear concept of the task, the team, and the technology—but I had no idea how hard it would be to raise the seven million dollars needed to charter the subs and produce the film.

I wrote a lengthy technical proposal and repeatedly updated it as the situation changed. It had little impact. I attended countless meetings that produced nothing but nodding silences. What follows is typical of the early phases of the project.

Ten months after my odyssey began I was in the office of Fred Klinkhammer, the outspoken president of IMAX. For twenty minutes he'd been telling me his company was reluctant to increase its participation in such a high-risk project. He was a big-boned, grey-haired man who made the air vibrate when he spoke.

"Russia is in chaos," he bellowed. "How can you be sure the Academy of Sciences will participate? And you don't have enough money. You're two million short."

"I've dived in one of the Russian subs to a depth deeper than *Titanic*. When they commit to a project, they deliver," I told him, and then, for the fifteenth time, I asked him if he would increase his investment.

He told me his company was committed to other projects.

"There is enormous public interest in *Titanic*," I countered. "Millions of people want to see the wreck up close. Only IMAX technology can give them a life-sized view. You'll get a big return on your investment."

Klinkhammer turned, stared out the window, and bit down hard on every word, "You're two million short."

I left the room more determined than ever. This was more than a film about a shipwreck; it was a one-of-a-kind project whose science and technology would change the way we think about the deep ocean. I called three of my friends who worked in the financial sector and they offered to help with bridge financing. I arranged for Sagalevich and his boss to fly to Toronto to meet Klinkhammer and other senior IMAX executives. I encouraged Stephen Low, an IMAX film director, to spend three days with *Mir* subs on their mother ship. Slowly, the fiscal tide began to turn. IMAX theatre managers in Toronto and Ottawa agreed to advance half a million dollars. At last, with most of the seven-million-dollar budget tentatively in place, Klinkhammer reluctantly gave us the green light.

Six months later we met Sagalevich and his big Russian ship in Bermuda, hauled tons of equipment up its gangway, and made two short dives to ensure our IMAX cameras and new lighting systems worked. Then we steamed north to the unmarked site where *Titanic* went down and dropped four acoustic beacons on the sea floor to guide the *Mirs* to the wreck. The weather stayed calm and we made the first five dives.

But a week into the expedition, in a small mid-deck cabin, I was confronted with a situation every leader dreads. I listened to the concerns of Al Giddings, Stephen Low, and Emory Kristof.

"As we were flying over the bow, he hit the davit."

"He can't hold the sub steady. We're missing key shots."

"If he continues to pilot like this, there's going to be a serious accident."

There was a long silence and then someone said, "We need you to tell Sagalevich he has to step back as lead pilot. Genya is younger and has better reflexes. We want him driving the camera sub."

My heart sank. Sagalevich was the co-designer of the *Mir* and had been the lead pilot since the day they were launched. How do you tell an old friend his performance is compromising the mission?

Two hours later I sat down with Sagalevich in his stateroom. I told him how much we appreciated the extraordinary effort he and his team were putting into the project. Then, as gently as possible, I outlined the problem.

He visibly stiffened and a palpable distance opened between us. No one tells a middle-aged Russian that after two hundred dives he is losing his touch with the machines he helped build. He conceded that this was his first time flying around a shipwreck laced with lethal hazards and unpredictable currents. Looking down at the floor, he agreed to my suggestion. The project came first. He would yield to the younger man and we would make the last dive together.

We made seventeen successful dives to the wreck. We carried out the first scientific study of *Titanic* and the debris field around it. We created an IMAX film seen by millions of people in dozens of countries. But during that half-hour conversation my friendship with Sagalevich began to unravel. Two years later, in part because of my failure to see what was happening, it was beyond repair.

When I took on the IMAX Titanic leadership challenge I was drawing on most of the sources of strength I've mentioned in this section: I was committed to the project's teams, technologies, and outcomes; I had used the clearest, most concise writing I was capable of to define what we were attempting to do and why it was important; and I had sought out the best mentors available in areas where I needed help.

However, as the setbacks and obstacles increased, it became harder to sustain my early levels of enthusiasm. I was forced to dig deep into my reservoirs of patience and persistence.

My mentors made the mission possible. Two IMAX executives became champions of the enterprise and gave me good advice on "how to play the corporate game." Al Giddings kept reminding me that this was more than a story about diving to the *Titanic*: it was a unique narrative of Russians and North Americans, former Cold War enemies, working together for the first time on a major deep-sea project. My battle-hardened shipmate Emory Kristof convinced *National Geographic* to participate and offered a steady stream of "damn-the-torpedoes" encouragement.

I've never been the perfect leader and this project was no exception. In spite of my best intentions I became impatient and even angry. I stamped my foot to stop an IMAX consultant coming aboard the ship and infecting the crew with her toxic personality. I grumbled loudly when Stephen Low announced he was going to build a mock-up of the interior of the *Mirs*, have the Russian and American sub teams act out imaginary confrontations and not let the audience in on the secret. And I failed to come up with the graceful words that might have explained the situation to Sagalevich without alienating him.

But in those two and a half years I learned more than I could have hoped for from my mentors, shipmates, and the ocean. Like so many hard challenges, the experience helped me to understand how important it is to take responsibility for your own mistakes and never repeat them. The experience helped build my character.

Leadership opportunities will present themselves to you in small places close to home or in big places far from home. Accept them with gusto. Help a group that is worthy and in need and you take another step toward wisdom.

REFLECTIONS ON SEEKING OPPORTUNITIES

FINDING LEADERSHIP opportunities is a real-time event. It comes alive the instant we make contact with a challenge or a mission that needs our support.

Leaders have a responsibility to look hard and often at how well they employ their leadership skills. And how effectively they weave them into a mosaic that inspires the team, the company, or the country.

There will be frequent opportunities for you to stand up and say what's on your mind. Prepare your words beforehand. Give them an inner logical structure that makes them easy to remember. Your centrepiece should be a dramatic story told with passion. Don't read your speech at the podium; stand in the centre of the stage, look at the roomful of faces, and give them both barrels.

Not everyone can be in the right place to step out on the moon. But everyone can find his own moon and get there by seeking more education. Education opened the doors for me and it's what can open doors for any young person today. Look ahead, try to assess your talents—make a good, honest appraisal—then add a little bit because you're going to grow. Most importantly, look for a challenge.

— BUZZ ALDRIN

Any man who has had what has been regarded as a great success must realize that the element of chance has played a great part in it. A man has to take advantage of his opportunities; but the opportunities have to come.

—TEDDY ROOSEVELT

Leadership often depends on good fortune. Not just in the development of leadership traits, but in having occasions arise where they can be applied.

Leadership, like mentorship, has a natural history. It is born, grows slowly, and creates a three-dimensional, living presence in the space between people. It takes time, talent, and tenacity. Leadership adapts. It is shaped by a kind of natural selection according to the challenges it faces and the team partners it acquires.

From its beginning the Occupy Wall Street movement was resolutely leaderless. As the movement spread from Zuccotti Park in New York to Los Angeles, Toronto and dozens of other cities, its thousands of participants focused our attention on "the 99 percent" and the economic hardships they faced. But their lack of leadership has diminished their effectiveness. They built summer camps filled with frustration and protest signs. They showed us "the people's mike" in action—the practice of a crowd repeating, verbatim, everything a speaker says. They confirmed they could organize their own food distribution and campsite cleanup. However, until they find leaders who articulate specific solutions to the problems, their main achievement will have been to show up, pitch their tents, and sleep through long, cold nights. In the words of the mayor of New York, Michael R. Bloomberg: "My personal view is, why don't you get out there and try to do something about the things you don't like, create the jobs that we are lacking, rather than just yell and scream. But if you want to yell and scream, we'll make sure you can do it."

Roméo Dallaire in his Senate office.

TRANSFORMING YOUR CHARACTER
MASTERY OF HONEST SELF-ASSESSMENT TO GENERATE AND REGENERATE THE ESSENTIAL TRAITS OF LEADERSHIP

ALL THE leaders I've met, worked with, and read about have had one thing in common. Along the way to becoming practitioners and masters of leadership, they transformed their character.

They acquired their own essential traits and consistently improved them. They read deeply, wrote and spoke with panache, and become more introspective. As their challenges evolved, they evolved with them.

For some reason, I saw the outlines of this process more clearly in military men and women. Because their lives depended on leadership every day, they lived and breathed it in ways we civilians can never know. From petty officers all the way up to captains and generals, most of them knew the strengths and weaknesses of their own character and the steps they needed to take to improve.

Before I travelled to Canada's military base in Kandahar, Afghanistan, I went to the Parliament Buildings in Ottawa to see a man whose capacity for transforming his character had helped inspire this book.

When I think of the consequences of the Rwandan genocide, I think of all those who died an agonizing death from machete wounds . . . I think of the more than 300,000 children who were killed, and of those children who became killers in a perversion of any culture's idea of childhood.

— ROMÉO DALLAIRE

I was sitting in his small Senate office talking to the man who wrote those words. Lieutenant General Roméo Dallaire had a shock of grey hair and a scrupulously groomed regimental moustache. "Today's military leaders," he told me, "must function in an environment that didn't exist a few years ago. Officers must be skilled warriors, but it's not enough. They need expertise and experience in things like anthropology, sociology, and philosophy to help them assist people in conflict and put the weapons as far back as possible."

Lieutenant General, now Senator, Dallaire served thirty-five years with the Canadian Forces. Late in 1993 he was given command of the United Nations Assistance Mission for Rwanda. The small nation of rolling hills in central Africa was in the middle of a civil war between the extremist Hutu government and a Tutsi rebel faction operating out of Uganda.

As the civil war exploded into the wide-scale slaughter of 800,000 Rwandans, Dallaire and his UN peacekeepers were abandoned by the world's major powers. They heard cries of agony and saw bodies lying on the roadside with severed limbs, shattered skulls, and gouged-out eyes. They saw death and rape squads—shouting men with bloody machetes—slaughtering unarmed women and children. Inside this circle of hell Dallaire discovered the metallic taste of his own fear.

The senator's sixty-four-year-old face was weathered and sculpted from witnessing one of the worst genocides in the twentieth century. In spite of this, the lines around his eyes hinted at a man who spent much of his time reading and writing. Nothing in his steady gaze suggested he had experienced savagery and horror beyond human comprehension.

"In today's realms of conflict you can't just cooperate or coordinate," he told me. "Or even collaborate. You need a new lexicon based on integration. A leader has to integrate different disciplines and create a new conceptual base. A leader has to be multidisciplined and multiskilled to grasp what can be done with diplomacy and military technologies."

His words were concise and confident because he'd said them many times to fellow senators, military officers, and university students. He spoke from a script embedded deep within his heart.

After he left Rwanda, the horrors he had seen hijacked the frontal lobes of his brain. He couldn't remember events in proper order. He struggled to connect disparate images. The brutal truth of thousands of lives snuffed out at random by men with crazed eyes spun round inside his head. He returned home broken, disillusioned, and suicidal.

I asked him how he survived the collapse of his moral universe.

"There was a time when I wanted to commit suicide because the traumas were too massive to live with. But slowly I began to realize that real change takes time. Ten, fifteen, perhaps twenty years will have to pass before we solve conflicts originating from the frictions of our differences. We can't change a culture, the impact of a religion, or the level of poverty right away. But we can make progress. There will be setbacks, but with a sustained effort we can diminish crimes against humanity. It may take centuries, but it can be done."

I glanced around the small office on the fourth floor of the Parliament Buildings. There was a photograph of Dallaire and two other UN peacekeepers, including his close friend Major

Brent Beardsley, carrying young Rwandans in their arms. There was a painting of seventeen Rwandan children standing beside the UN commander, their eyes wide with wonder and anticipation. The images suggested where Dallaire found his redemption. It was in his love for humanity. It began with a profound understanding of mortality and the preciousness and responsibility of being alive.

When he entered the room Dallaire had shaken my hand and apologized for being late. He spoke with an awkward tenderness, saying he had been at a cabin north of the city trying to finish his new book on child soldiers. He was behind schedule, still wrestling with the final draft.

The book, *They Fight Like Soldiers, They Die Like Children*, begins in Rwanda where he first saw children engaged in warfare. He describes young boys as "an increasingly popular weapon system that requires negligible technology, is simple to sustain, has unlimited versatility and incredible capacity for loyalty and barbarism." There are more than two hundred and fifty thousand child soldiers fighting in conflicts around the world and Dallaire is adamant about changing this. "The ultimate focus of the rest of my life is to eradicate the use of child soldiers and eliminate the thought of using children as instruments of war."

I asked him about tomorrow's leaders and the issues they face.

"Twenty- and thirty-year-olds are pushing the old generations aside. The revolution in communications has erased boundaries and barriers from their mindset. They converse with someone in Moscow and Rio as if they're next door. They see the planet as a tiny blue sphere in the middle of the universe. They know that we'll soon be able to talk to the whole planet. They're part of a new era where concepts like human rights—that *all* humans *are* human—make profound, enduring sense."

The wellspring of Dallaire's greatness was that he wove his

deep leadership traits into a transformative character. He had returned from a heart-of-darkness journey with his morality ruptured and memory broken to discover that for all its hellishness, genocide was temporary and the hope for anti-violence was universal and permanent. He had figured out who he was and what he stood for. He knew he was in the midst of a long war, but he was going to win it whatever it took. He was going to win it with courage, kindness, and honesty. He was living confirmation that old lions are still lions.

REFLECTIONS ON TRANSFORMING YOUR CHARACTER

CHARACTER—who you are, what you know, how you feel, what you've done, and what you can do—defines the dimensions of your leadership.

Character is the ship that carries you through the turbulence of choice and judgment. Its keel is physical robustness; its hull is mental resilience. Among its crossbeams are strategic imagination, fierce ingenuity, and resolute courage. Its cargo includes blood trust and team genius. Its pilothouse contains your compass of core values.

As the containment vessel for our hopes, fears, visions, and values, character is fragile. Most of the time it operates below the surface of what is seen and heard. It contains tensions that are hard to control. To operate for long periods at peak performance it requires rigorous self-assessment, constant correction, and honest humility.

To be truly transformed through knowledge and experience takes ten years, ten thousand hours of learning, experimenting, improving what works, changing what doesn't, practising new techniques, and repeating this process over and over, until both knowledge and experience are mastered.

The characteristic of heroism is its persistency . . . when you have chosen your part abide by it. If you would serve your brother because it is fit for you to serve him, do not take back your words when you find that prudent people do not commend you.

—RALPH WALDO EMERSON

Transformative leaders write well, speak well, and are willing to take decisive action. To transform themselves and those around them, they're ready to act in the face of multiple, manifest uncertainties. They are an inspiration to dream big and live large.

Solitude, silence, and stamina—these are part of the daily fare of being a leader.

"A human being," says Nobel Prize–winner Octavio Paz, "is never what he is but the self that he seeks." If we're fortunate and focused, we grow in complexity, understanding, and humility. The depth and degree of this change influences our colleagues, community, and children. As a dynamic process, transformation works both ways.

The author during Sealab III.

FINAL REFLECTIONS

A FEW months after Jim Cameron brought us to Washington to consider technical options for BP's oil spill, I flew to New Orleans and then drove south toward the Gulf of Mexico. The road sliced through the Louisiana tidelands, an endless blur of swamp-forest, bay heads, and tidal marsh winding across the Mississippi Delta until it ended at Grand Isle, a long barrier island.

Since the late 1800s, the island had been repeatedly hammered by tropical storms and hurricanes. Every eight years or so, blistering winds and a high tide blow a storm surge across the island. Today, its fifteen hundred souls live in wooden houses built on thick hurricane pilings.

You can't talk about Grand Isle without talking about the fishing and the beaches. Most of its inhabitants make their living as shrimpers, fishers, and charter-boat captains. For decades, thousands of sport fishermen have been drawn to the more than two hundred species of fish including tarpon, tuna, and dolphin in the Gulf of Mexico. Grand Isle's wide, well-maintained beaches are a perennial summer destination for hundreds of communities in south Louisiana.

The day I arrived was flame-thrower hot, and breathing the air was like breathing soup. As I drove into town I saw dozens of hand-painted signs on both sides of the road saying:

WELCOME TO GRAND OIL
YOU KILLED THE GULF—BP—AND OUR WAY OF LIFE
HOW THE HELL ARE WE GOING TO FEED OUR KIDS?

The streets and marinas were empty and the air smelled of burned saltmarsh. The only people on the beach were wearing orange vests and white haz-mat suits. A chain of front-end loaders were digging near the water's edge and hauling the sand over to a hundred-foot-long black scrubber filling the air with diesel smoke.

I found a flashing Budweiser sign, opened the door, and took a seat at the bar. In a haze of stale beer and working sweat, a shrimp fisherman with bloodshot eyes told me, "My boat has been tied to the pier for ten weeks." I mentioned the sand scrubber working to restore the beach. He told me that the oil went deep under the sand and couldn't be scrubbed out. Like everyone else in town, he was angry, frustrated, and suspicious.

Just before sunset I walked across the street to the beach and looked south to where the burned-out hulk of the *Deepwater Horizon* lay under a mile of seawater.

So much had changed since my first trip here forty years earlier. As the medical director of Ocean Systems I'd raced down the highway from Morgan City in an old pickup truck to treat a diver stricken with a near-fatal case of the bends. He was one of thirty-five raw-boned divers working on offshore drilling platforms and undersea pipelines. They were cool, competent men, loud-laughing and serious with a natural caution. Their hands were cross-hatched with barnacle cuts. When they donned their heavy gear and dived into the ocean, they spent hours, sometimes days, underwater, repairing blowout preventers and replacing pipelines. They knew injury and death at sea in its most surprising and painful aspects. Their supervisors were among my early leadership mentors.

These were tough men educated by hard experience. They were not sweeping thinkers, but they were rigorously honest about judging themselves. They made sensitive discriminations about people and circumstances. They had learned to operate within the constraints life imposed on them without complaining. They had a delicate understanding of what was required at a given place and time. Like the sailors and carpenters of centuries past, they were proud to be judged by their craftsmanship.

Those men, older now, must scarcely recognize the world we live in today. We've cut down too many trees, diverted too many rivers, eliminated too many species, consumed too much energy, and added too many layers to Earth's carbon dioxide blanket. Seven billion people now live on a planet where sea levels are rising, food prices are up, super storms are increasing, energy prices are soaring, people are being displaced from their homes, and floods and droughts are setting records. Governments all around the world are threatened by the convergence of it all. According to the men and women who think hard about these things, our economic system of unending growth and our natural system of staying within limits are violently colliding.

My shipmates of forty years ago would not recognize this world but would recognize the origins of the problem. The first rule of working in a lethal environment is that *you do not mess with your life-support system.*

THE FOLLOWING morning I drove to Oceaneering International in Morgan City and spent two days with the soft-spoken men who operate the remotely operated subs—ROVs—that helped cap BP's runaway well. Their five-million-dollar, seven-ton machines had five cameras, six thrusters, and two mechanical steel arms that could push and pull, grab and twist. These remotely operated "flying tool boxes" performed hundreds of tasks from bolting flanges to inspecting blowout preventers and cutting pipes.

The pilots were thirty- and forty-year-olds from Texas, Louisiana, and Mississippi, the older version of guys you'd expect to see playing video games. But they did much more than sit at control consoles. They worked in a world of heaving decks, slippery stairwells, overheated generators, and cables under tension. They fought with the pressure and saltwater corrosion attacking their complex machines. They were technical troubleshooters, self-taught engineers who knew every humming inch of their electro-mechanical avatars. They could fly them and fix them in their sleep.

Oceaneering had fifty pilots and twenty ROVs working on the eighty-seven-day blowout in non-stop twelve-hour shifts. They spent fifteen thousand hours beneath the sea as "the eyes and hands" for almost every task. They knew anxiety, exhaustion. They knew the whole world was watching. They tried to activate the blowout preventer; they cut and cleared the riser and helped position the cap that kept the oil from flowing.

For the exhausted BP managers, Oceaneering's flying tool boxes were the Seventh Cavalry on rotating propellers. During those fifteen thousand hours their pilots demonstrated an elegant fusion of fierce ingenuity, team genius, high-empathy communication, and hot-zone humour.

During the drive back to New Orleans I reflected on some of the things the ocean and other lethal environments have taught me about leadership.

Leadership is very much like the ocean: complex, multi-layered, and filled with large, unexplored areas.

Great leaders are endowed with a sense of wonder—and humility. Their respect for the unexpected and unfamiliar is central to their character. According to the writer Edward Rothstein:

"Wonder is not puzzlement, bewilderment or confusion. But it is also not satisfaction, completion or understanding. It is more open ended, even a little unsettling. There is an element of calm, poised detachment . . . but also a restless amazement. In the wake of wonder, we are literally moved. We cannot remain still. We are spurred to exploration."

It is from numberless diverse acts of courage and belief that human history is shaped. Each time a man stands up for an ideal, or acts to improve the lot of others, or strikes out against injustice, he sends forth a tiny ripple of hope, and crossing each other from a million different centers of energy and daring, those ripples build a current that can sweep down the mightiest walls of oppression and resistance.

— ROBERT F. KENNEDY, SOUTH AFRICA, 1966

We try to define it. We have discussions about whether or not it's innate, whether or not it's a learned response, whether it's something you develop over time. And I think that's tremendously important, because without deliberate thought about what it takes to be an effective leader, an effective commander, we're not going to be able to prepare future generations. But there's a danger. I worry that by defining it we make it too small. Effective leadership is so much wider and broader than anyone else can define for you and it comes in different shapes and forms. So the moment we think we can put it in a little box and understand and define it then we've failed as leaders, because we've failed to both test ourselves and try to move forward. Leadership is something that needs to be tested, needs to be developed, but we should never be happy that we've actually defined it. It will always be broader than we think it is.

— MAJOR GENERAL MIKE DAY

LIST OF PHOTOGRAPHS

Powerful Presentations

Physical Robustness

Hot-Zone Humour

Mental Resilience

Strategic Imagination

High-Empathy Communication

Blood Trust

Fierce Ingenuity

Team Genius

Resolute Courage

Warrior's Honour

PART THREE: Navigating Towards Leadership

Making the Commitment

Commanding the Language

Building a Library

Finding Mentors

Seeking Opportunities

Transforming Your Character

Final Reflections

SELECTED REFERENCES

SEARCHING FOR THE ESSENCE OF LEADERSHIP

Cameron, James, and Members of an Ad Hoc Deep Ocean Group. *Considering Technical Options for Controlling the BP Blowout in the Gulf of Mexico*. Washington, D.C., June 2010.

ACCIDENTAL APPRENTICE

Craven, John P. *The Silent War: The Cold War Battle Beneath the Sea*. New York: Simon and Schuster, 2001.

Cronkite, Walter. *A Reporter's Life*. New York: Knopf, 1996.

David Halberstam. *The Powers That Be*. New York: Knopf, 1979.

Kennedy, John F. Address to Rice University, Houston, TX. September 12, 1962.

Link, Marion Clayton. *Windows in the Sea*. Washington, D.C.: Smithsonian Institution Press, 1973.

Link, Marion Clayton. *Sea Diver: A Quest for History Under the Sea*. Miami: University of Miami Press, 1964.

MacInnis, Joe. *Breathing Underwater: The Quest to Live in the Sea*. Toronto: Penguin Books Canada, 2004.

ACCIDENTAL LEADER

Jovanovic, Bané. *28° Above Below*. Montreal: National Film Board of
    Canada, 1973. Directed by Bané Jovanovic and Ken Page. Film.

Berton, Pierre. *The Arctic Grail: The Quest for the Northwest Passage and
    the North Pole 1818-1909*. Toronto: McClelland & Stewart, 1988.

MacInnis, Joe. "Diving Beneath Arctic Ice." *National Geographic*,
    August 1973.

MacInnis, Joe. "Exploring a 140-Year-Old Ship Under Arctic Ice."
    National Geographic, July 1983.

MacInnis, Joe. "Polar Seas" in *The Ocean Realm*. Washington, D.C.:
    National Geographic Society, 1978.

MacInnis, Joe. *The Land That Devours Ships: The Search for the
    Breadalbane*. Toronto: CBC Enterprises, 1985.

MacInnis, Joseph, Patrick Watson and Margaret Pettigrew. *The Land
    That Devours Ships*. Montreal: National Film Board of Canada,
    1984. Directed by Bill Mason. Film.

SERIOUS STUDENT

Flannery, Tim. *The Weather Makers: How We Are Changing
    the Climate and What It Means for Earth*. New York:
    HarperCollins, 2006.

Friedman, Thomas L. *Hot, Flat, and Crowded: Why We Need
    a Green Revolution—and How It Can Renew America*.
    New York: Farrar, Straus and Giroux, 2008.

Homer-Dixon, Thomas. *The Upside of Down: Catastrophe, Creativity
    and the Renewal of Civilization*. Toronto: Vintage Canada, 2007.

Karl, Thomas R., Jerry M. Melillo and Thomas C. Peterson, eds.
    Global Climate Change Impacts in the United States, Cambridge,
    U.K.: Cambridge University Press, 2009.

MacInnis, Joe. *Fire in the Ocean: The Story of the Komsomolets*.
    Unpublished.

Maas, Peter. *Crude World: The Violent Twilight of Oil*. New York: Alfred A. Knopf, 2009.

Monbiot, George. *Heat: How to Stop the Planet From Burning*. Toronto: Doubleday Canada, 2006.

COOL COMPETENCE

Bradbury, Ray. "An Impatient Gulliver Above Our Roofs." *Life*, November 24, 1967. (Richard F. Gordon, Jr. quoted.)

Carpenter, Scott, and Kris Stoever. *For Spacious Skies: The Uncommon Journey of a Mercury Astronaut*. New York: Harcourt, 2002.

Lawrence, Richard Russell, ed. *Space Exploration and Disasters*. New York: Carroll and Graf, 2005.

Wolfe, Tom. *The Right Stuff*. New York: Farrar, Straus and Giroux, 1979.

POWERFUL PRESENTATIONS

Greene, Richard, with Florie Brizel. *Words That Shook the World: 100 Years of Unforgettable Speeches and Events*. New York: Prentice Hall Press, 2001.

Spicer, Keith. *The Winging It Logic System: How To Speak Confidently Without Notes*. Toronto: Doubleday Canada, 1984.

PHYSICAL ROBUSTNESS

Sewell, Kenneth. *All Hands Down: The True Story of the Soviet Attack on the USS Scorpion*. New York: Simon and Schuster, 2008.

Shackleton, Sir Ernest. *The Heart of the Antarctic*. Philadelphia: J.B. Lippencott, 1909.

Sontag, Sherry, and Christopher Drew. *Blind Man's Bluff: The Untold Story of American Submarine Espionage*. New York: PublicAffairs, 1998.

Spufford, Francis. *I May Be Some Time: Ice and the English Imagination.* New York: Picador, 1997.

HOT-ZONE HUMOUR

Bond, George F. *Papa Topside: The Sealab Chronicles of Capt. George F. Bond, USN.* Annapolis: Naval Institute Press, 1993.

Craven, John P. *The Silent War: The Cold War Battle Beneath the Sea.* New York: Simon and Schuster, 2001.

Gonzales, Laurence. *Deep Survival: Who Lives, Who Dies, and Why.* New York: W. W. Norton & Company, 2003.

Gorman, James. "Scientists Hint at Why Laughter Feels So Good." *New York Times,* September 13, 2011. (Robin Dunbar quoted.)

Pink, Daniel. *A Whole New Mind: Why Right Brainers Will Rule the Future.* New York: Riverhead, 2005.

MENTAL RESILIENCE

Axworthy, Thomas S., and Pierre Elliott Trudeau, eds. *Toward A Just Society: The Trudeau Years.* Toronto: Penguin Books Canada, 1990.

Barack Obama, interview by Steve Kroft, *60 Minutes,* CBS, May 8, 2011.

Trudeau, Pierre Elliott. *Memoirs.* Toronto: McClelland & Stewart, 1993.

STRATEGIC IMAGINATION

Joseph Conrad. *A Personal Record.* New York and London: Harper & Brothers Publishers, 1912.

Gonzales, Laurence. *Everyday Survival: Why Smart People Do Stupid Things.* New York: W.W. Norton and Company, 2008.

Ripley, Amanda. *The Unthinkable: Who Survives When Disaster Strikes and Why.* New York: Crown Archetype, 2008.

HIGH-EMPATHY COMMUNICATION

Doidge, Norman. *The Brain That Changes Itself: Stories of Personal Triumph from the Frontiers of Brain Science*. New York: Penguin Books, 2007.

BLOOD TRUST

Bennett, William J. *The Book of Virtues: A Treasury of Great Moral Stories*. New York: Simon and Schuster, 1993.

Sagalevich, Anatoly M. with Paul T. Isley. *The Deep: Voyages to Titanic and Beyond*. Redondo Beach, CA: Botanical Press, 2009.

Sagalevich, Anatoly M. *Mysteries of the Deeps: From the Depths of Lake Baikal to the Ocean Floor*. Moscow: Progress Publishers, 1989.

Smith, Hedrick. *The New Russians*. New York: Random House, 1990.

FIERCE INGENUITY

Hallowell, Edward M. *Shine: Using Brain Science to Get the Best from Your People*. Boston: Harvard Business Review Press, 2011.

MacInnis, Joe. *James Cameron's Aliens of the Deep: Voyages to the Strange World of the Deep Ocean*. Washington, D.C.: National Geographic Books, 2004.

MacInnis, Joe. *Titanic Dreams: Reflections on the Discovery, Exploration and Salvage of the World's Most Famous Shipwreck*. Self-published, 2007.

TEAM GENIUS

Sawyer, Keith. *Group Genius: The Creative Power of Collaboration.* New York: Basic Books, 2007.

Steve Jobs, interview by Betsy Morris, CNNMoney, last modified March 7, 2008. http://money.cnn.com/galleries/2008/fortune/0803/gallery.jobsqna.fortune/7.html

RESOLUTE COURAGE

Aldrin, Buzz. *A Unified Space Vision: What Human Spaceflight Can Do For America.* 8 July 2009. Personal communication.

Aldrin, Buzz, with Ken Abraham. *Magnificent Desolation: The Long Journey Home from the Moon.* New York: Crown Archetype, 2009.

Chaikin, Andrew. *A Man on the Moon; The Voyages of the Apollo Astronauts.* New York: Penguin Books, 1994.

Hedges, Chris. *War is a Force That Gives Us Meaning.* New York: Anchor Books, 2003.

Lord Moran. *The Anatomy of Courage.* New York: Basic Books, 2007.

WARRIOR'S HONOUR

Kolenda, Christopher. *Leadership: The Warrior's Art.* Carlisle, PA: Army War College Foundation Press, 2001.

Low, Colin. *Arctic IV.* Montreal: National Film Board of Canada, 1975. Directed by James Domville. Film.

Moore, Harold G. (Lt. Gen.). *We Were Soldiers Once . . . and Young: Ia Drang –The Battle That Changed the War in Vietnam.* New York: Random House, 1992.

Moore, Harold G. (Lt. Gen.). *We Are Soldiers Still: A Journey Back to the Battlefields of Vietnam.* New York: Harper, 2008.

NAVIGATING TOWARD LEADERSHIP

Maslow, Abraham. "A Theory of Human Motivation," *Psychological Review* 50 no. 4 (1943): 370-96.

MAKING THE COMMITMENT

Brando, Marlon, with Robert Lindsay, *Songs My Mother Taught Me.* New York: Random House, 1994.

Chopra, Deepak. *The Soul of Leadership: Unlocking Your Potential for Greatness.* New York: Harmony, 2010.

Domville, James. *Sub-Igloo.* Montreal: National Film Board of Canada, 1973. Directed by James Domville and Joseph MacInnis. Film.

Dyer, Gwynne. *Climate Wars.* Toronto: Random House Canada, 2008.

Jobs, Steve. Address at Stanford University's 114th Commencement on June 12, 2005. http://www.youtube.com/watch?v=UF8uR6Z6KLc.

Yevtushenko, Yevgeny. *Fatal Half Measures: The Culture of Democracy in the Soviet Union.* New York: Little, Brown, 1991.

COMMANDING THE LANGUAGE

Cheever, John. Accepting the National Medal of Literature, 1982.

Gardner, Howard. *Leading Minds: An Anatomy of Leadership.* New York: Basic Books, 1995.

Graves, Robert, and Alan Hodge. *The Reader Over Your Shoulder: A Handbook for Writers of English Prose.* New York: Vintage Books, 1979.

Hitchens, Christopher. "Unspoken Truths." *Vanity Fair,* June 2011.

Melville, Herman. *The Letters of Herman Melville.* New Haven: Yale University Press, 1960.

Newman, Peter C. *Here Be Dragons: Telling Tales of People, Passion and Power.* Toronto: McClelland & Stewart, 2004.

Safire, William, and Leonard Safire. *Good Advice on Writing:*
Great Quotations from Writers Past and Present on How to
Write Well. New York: Simon and Schuster, 1992.

Shenker, Israel. "E. B. White: Notes and Comment by Author."
New York Times, July 11, 1969.

Strunk, William Jr., and E.B. White. *The Elements of Style.*
New York: MacMillan, 1979.

Twain, Mark. Letter to George Bainton, October 15, 1888.

BUILDING A LIBRARY

Baron-Cohen, Simon. *The Science of Evil: On Empathy and the*
Origins of Cruelty. New York: Basic Books, 2011.

Brooks, David. "Social Animal: How the new sciences of human nature
can help make sense of life." *The New Yorker,* January 17, 2011.

Gee, James Paul. *What Video Games Have to Teach Us About*
Learning and Literacy. New York: Palgrave MacMillan, 2003.

Goleman, Daniel. *Emotional Intelligence: Why It Can Matter More*
Than IQ. New York: Bantam Books, 1995.

Gore, Al. *Our Choice: A Plan to Solve the Climate Crisis.* Emmaus,
PA: Rodale, 2009.

Heilpern, John. "An editor and a Gentleman," *Vanity Fair,*
November 2011.

Howard, Gardner. *Leading Minds: An Anatomy of Leadership.* New
York: Basic Books, 1995.

Kolenda, Christopher (author-editor). *Leadership: The Warrior's Art.*

Leanne, Shel. *Say It Like Obama.* New York: McGraw-Hill, 2009.

Phillips, Donald T. *Martin Luther King, Jr., On Leadership:*
Inspiration and Wisdom for Challenging Times. New York:
Business Plus, 1998.

Roosevelt, Theodore. *Theodore Roosevelt: An Autobiography.* New
York: MacMillan, 1913.

Strock, James. *Theodore Roosevelt on Leadership*. New York:
Three Rivers Press, 2001.

Sutton, Robert I. *The No Asshole Rule: Building a Civilized
Workplace and Surviving One That Isn't*. New York: Business
Plus, 2007.

FINDING MENTORS

Couric, Katie. *The Best Advice I Ever Got: Lessons from Extraordinary
Lives*. New York: Random House, 2011.

McCain, John, with Mark Salter. *Character Is Destiny: Inspiring
Stories Every Young Person Should Know and Every Adult Should
Remember*. New York: Random House, 2005.

Wooden, John. *A Game Plan for Life: The Power of Mentoring*.
Bloomsbury, 2009.

SEEKING OPPORTUNITIES

Goodal, Jane. *Hope For Animals and Their World: How Endangered
Species Are Being Rescued from the Brink*. New York: Grand
Central Publishing, 2009.

Goodall, Jane, with Phillip Berman. *Reason For Hope: A Spiritual
Journey*. New York: Warner Books, 2000.

Roosevelt, Theodore. Address at the Cambridge Union, Cambridge,
England, May 26, 1910.

Westly, Frances. *Getting to Maybe: How the World Is Changed*.
Toronto: Vintage Canada, 2007.

TRANSFORMATIVE CHARACTER

Dallaire, Roméo. *Shake Hands with the Devil: The Failure of Humanity in Rwanda*. Toronto: Random House Canada, 2003.

Dallaire, Roméo. *They Fight Like Soldiers, They Die Like Children: The Global Quest to Eradicate the Use of Child Soldiers*, Toronto: Random House, 2010.

Emerson, Ralph Waldo. "Heroism," 1841.

Finkel, David. *The Good Soldiers*. New York: Farrar, Strauss and Giroux, 2009.

Harari, Oren. *The Leadership Secrets of Colin Powell*. New York: McGraw-Hill, 2002.

Junger, Sebastian. *War*. New York: HarperCollins, 2010.

Paz, Octavio. *The Double Flame: Love and Eroticism*. New York: Houghton Mifflin Harcourt, 1995.

Ripley, Amanda. *The Unthinkable: Who Survives When Disaster Strikes and Why*. New York: Crown, 2008.

FINAL REFLECTIONS

Kennedy, Robert F. Day of Affirmation Address, University of Capetown, Capetown, South Africa, June 6, 1966.

Rothstein, Edward. "Wonders of Science at the Golden Gate," *New York Times*, November 3, 2009.

ACKNOWLEDGEMENTS

This book is a love letter to all my children and grandchildren. It is also a salute to all those men and women who have made a lifelong commitment to social justice and protection of the natural world. It was made possible by:

My wife, Debby, who has given me her loving support since the beginning.

Louise Dennys, publisher of Knopf Canada, whose sustained encouragement brought this book into being, and Paul Taunton, my clear-eyed and always helpful editor. Additional thanks to Anne Collins, Marion Garner, Nicola Makoway, Deirdre Molina, Carla Kean, Andrew Roberts, Amanda Lewis, Doris Cowan, Liba Berry, Terra Page, and everyone at Knopf Canada.

Jim Cameron, who invited me to join his deep sea expeditions and film sets and gave me intimate views of lightning-hot leadership in action.

Scott Carpenter, Buzz Aldrin, Kathy Sullivan, Megan McArthur, Dave Williams, and Julie Payette, who helped me understand what it takes to ride rockets into space.

Colonel Bill Bentley at the Canadian Forces Leadership Institute and Colonel Bernd Horn, Major General Mike Day, Petty Officer Kerry Houghton, Brigadier General Dean Milner, Chief Warrant Officer Stu Hartnell, Brigadier General Jonathan Vance, Commander Rich Feltham, Major Steve Nolan, Dr. Harold Coombs, Commander Mike Mooze, Lieutenant General Hal Moore, and Melanie Davis, for mentoring me in the complex contours of warrior leadership.

Paul Kennedy, Bernie Lucht, and Dave Field who turned my interviews in Afghanistan into a one-hour radio special— *Leadership Under Fire*—for CBC's *Ideas*.

Howie Gold and Steve McDonald at Creative Post who turned my interviews in Afghanistan and HMCS *Toronto* into a leadership video—*Warrior's Honour*—for the Canadian Forces.

The University of Toronto, the University of Waterloo, the World Wildlife Fund, and the Nature Conservancy, for letting me express some of my early ideas to their audiences. And my students at Harbor Branch Oceanographic Institution and Carlton University's EMBA Course for their provocative questions and answers.

Darryl Rynquest and his teammates at Oceaneering International who showed me how their remotely operated vehicles helped cap BP's runaway oil well in the Gulf of Mexico.

And finally, to all the men and women on James Cameron's DEEPSEA Challenge Expedition who displayed such grace under pressure.

INDEX

Glenn, John, 21, 47, 50

Goethe, Johann Wolfgang von, 166

Goleman, Daniel, 182–83

Gonzales, Laurence, 76, 187

Goodall, Jane, 6, 42

Google, 161

Gorbachev, Mikhail, 164, 165, 167

Gordon, Richard F., Jr., 51

Gore, Al, 61

Grand Isle (Louisiana), 215–16

Graves, Bill, 174

Greater Lamashur Bay (US Virgin Islands), 79

Greene, Richard, 61

Greenpeace, 41, 110

Grosvenor, Melville Bell, 19

Group Genius (Sawyer), 187

Grunsfeld, John, 151–52

Gulf of Mexico, 1–2, 3, 18, 30, 215

Halberstam, David, 23

Halliburton Company, 3

Hallowell, Edward M., 123

Harbor Branch Oceanographic, 1

Havel, Vaclav, 60

Hayward, Tony, 2

Hedges, Chris, 139

Hemingway, Ernest, 182

Hitchens, Christopher, 176

HMCS *Toronto*, 5, 154, 170, 195

HMS *Breadalbane*. See *Breadalbane*

Hobaugh, Charlie, 91

Homer-Dixon, Thomas, 6, 41–42

Hot, Flat, and Crowded (Friedman), 42

Houghton, Kerry, 195

Hubble (space telescope), 57, 149–50, 151–52

Hungary, 164

Hutu tribe, 208

IBM Golden Circle, 60

IBM, 49

Ideas (radio show), 93

IMAX Titanic expedition, 199–203

Indian Ocean, 118

Ingenuity Gap, The (Homer-Dixon), 41

International Space Station, 5, 43, 48, 89, 90, 150

Invictus (film), 185

Jess, Pete, 33

Jobs, Steve, 130, 168

Johnson Space Center (Houston), 90

Johnson, Greg, 151

Johnson, Lyndon B., 24

Jones, John Paul, 65

Kamchatka (undersea canyon), 14, 110

Kandahar (Afghanistan), 5, 207

Kennedy, John F., 20–21, 23, 56, 136–37

DR. JOE MACINNIS is a physician-scientist and author who studies leadership in high-risk environments—*deep leadership*—and how its components can make us better leaders. He's led ten research expeditions under the ice of the Arctic Ocean, spent time with astronauts who built the International Space Station, and interviewed Canadian Forces in Afghanistan. In 2012, MacInnis was the electronic journalist and backup physician for James Cameron's *Deepsea Challenge* expedition. During the thirteen dives he kept a daily journal and took video and still photographs. His journal was posted on the National Geographic website www.deepseachallenge. MacInnis has delivered keynote presentations on leadership to IBM, Microsoft, General Electric and the U.S. Naval Academy. The author of ten books, his research has earned him six honorary degrees and his nation's highest honour, the Order of Canada.

www.drjmacinnis.com

A NOTE ABOUT THE TYPE

Deep Leadership is set in Electra, designed in 1935 by William Addison Dwiggins. A popular face for book-length work since its release, Electra is noted for its evenness and high legibility in both text sizes and display settings.